A KNIGHT AND HIS HORSE

By the same author:
A KNIGHT AND HIS ARMOR
A KNIGHT IN BATTLE
A KNIGHT AND HIS CASTLE
A KNIGHT AND HIS WEAPONS
DARK AGE WARRIOR
THE ARCHAEOLOGY OF WEAPONS
THE SWORD IN THE AGE OF CHIVALRY

About the Author

Ewart Oakeshott was born in 1916. He began collecting swords while still in school at Dulwich, and has since built up a superb collection, specializing in the medieval period. His books include *The Archaeology of Weapons, European Weapons and Armour, The Sword in the Age of Chivalry,* and the acclaimed "Knight" series. He always brings to his books a wide and deep knowledge of his subject, and a witty and pithy style. The *Times Educational Supplement* rightly called him "one of those rarely gifted researchers who combine exhaustive investigation with absorbing enthusiasm." Oakeshott (and three friends) founded the Arms and Armour Society, a concern with a worldwide membership. His home is in Ely, close to Cambridge, England.

A KNIGHT
AND HIS HORSE

Second Edition

EWART OAKESHOTT F.S.A.
Illustrated by the author

Dufour Editions

First published 1962,
this revised second edition published 1998

Published in the United States of America by
Dufour Editions Inc.,
Chester Springs, Pennsylvania 19425

ISBN 0-8023-1297-7

Library of Congress Cataloging-in-Publication Data

Oakeshott, R. Ewart.
    A knight and his horse / Ewart Oakeshott ; illustrated by the
author. – 2nd ed.
       p. cm.
    Originally published: Chester Springs, PA : Lutterworth Press, 1962.
    Summary: Describes the horses used by knights in the Middle Ages,
as well as the equipment and weapons they used in battle.
    ISBN 0-8023-1297-7
    1. Armor, Medieval--Juvenile literature. 2. Knights and knighthood
Juvenile literature. 3. Horses--Juvenile literature.
[1. Knights and knighthood. 2. Armor, Medieval. 3. Horses.]
I. Title.
U800.O33   1998
623.4'41--dc21   98-32049
                                               CIP
                                               AC

Printed and bound in the
United States of America

Contents

In grateful memory of my father,
RONALD LEWIS OAKESHOTT
who (among many other things)
taught me to joust

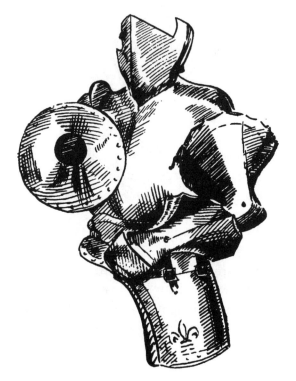

Fig. 1. "Double pieces," made for Francis I of France by Jorg Seusenhofer of Innsbruck in 1539/40, consisting of vamplate, grandguard (covering left side of visor, left shoulder and chest) pasguard (for the left elbow), manifer (main-de-fer) for the left hand, and left reinforcing tasset.

The Horse

It is inconceivable to think of a medieval knight not having a horse; the two go hand in hand, the one working in unison with the other, helping to define and clarify the other's role in the medieval scheme of things. Though we can accept the idea of a knight fighting on foot or assaulting a wall from a ladder - or even of a knight unhorsed - his mount is nevertheless there in the background. A knight with no horse would be hardly a knight at all; as a fighter, he would be ridiculous, absurd, useless, just as a modern army tank would be wholly ineffective without a motor. As important and essential as the medieval horse was to knighthood, the question remains: What kind of horse was it?

The popular idea is of a great ponderous cart-horse, standing about seventeen hands, onto which the armored warrior had to be hoisted with a crane. This notion is utterly wrong; the crane business is pure nonsense, invented by a modern theatrical producer as a funny gag. No, the medieval war-horse was a good strong working horse, like the old bus horses that few people remember now. The nearest thing to the medieval horse these days is perhaps the heavy hunter or large show-jumping horse: in Poland not too long ago middleweight horses exactly the right type for a medieval knight were still in use.

Several types of riding horse existed in the latter part of the Middle Ages (we must remember that the entire period covers a relatively long stretch of human history, from about A.D. 449 until 1500). Some useful literary references can help us sort out the different kinds of horses. A *chanson* of 1360, for instance, provides this useful overview of the horse scene (the verse is roughly translated here in prose): "There are three kinds of horse: for the joust they are called destriers, tall and majestic and with great

Fig. 2. Knight on his destrier, about 1260-1340

strength; the next are called coursers. They are more for use in war, and are lighter; and then there are rounseys. And the lowest are common horses; these are used for laboring, and are of a poor breed" (Eustach Deschamps, 1360).

The descriptions here are clear enough. The destrier's appearance is specified like his function, and never varies. Wherever we find reference to destriers—whether in

Fig. 3. Sergeant in a rounsey, about 1260-1340. (the arms and armor of Sergeants varied hardly at all between about 1250 and 1400)

poem, military ordinance, inventory, or will—it is the same in all parts of Europe. He is the Great Horse, the knightly horse *par excellence.* His high breeding and careful training are the mark of his caste, and his main function is to bear his master in the joust, the noblest and most admired exercise among all the knightly arts of combat. For the harder, longer, and less splendid work of war, the courser was the preferred mount, less valuable and lighter than the destrier and probably trained in a less specific way.

11

The rounsey was as strong as the war-horse, or nearly as strong, but of no particular breeding. He served as a cavalry horse for non-knightly men-at-arms (called in those days sergeants), or as a riding horse simply to get about on.

A French Royal Ordinance of 1265, setting limits on the amount of money people of various classes could spend on things, mandated that no squire, not even of noble blood and considerable wealth, could buy an ambling rounsey worth more than fifteen livres or a trotting one worth more than twenty (see Appendix B).

Except for the destrier, these horses were named according to their gait; the names are French in origin. The courser is a running horse and the ambler

Fig. 4. A nobleman hunting on a palfrey, about 1440

ambles. Ambling is a natural gait, like the running of deer, and can vary from the speed of a fast walk to a canter. The ambler provides a smooth and easy ride, suitable for traveling and similar to the gait of horses ridden by cattlemen in Australia and

Fig. 5. A lady on a jennet, about 1380

America who have to spend long days in the saddle. The trot is a gait neither entirely natural nor especially comfortable. A horse has to be trained and bred to trot, just as a rider has to learn to rise to it; of course, the trot gives a smarter appearance than an amble. A well-managed horse, lifting his feet up well and riding gallantly at a trot, is a proud and splendid sight. But a trot is not effective unless the rider, trained well, rises to it. To sit in the saddle and jiggle gives an impression of discomfort. Of course, medieval knights would never have tried to trot in armor. The weight of their equipment would have made riding in such fashion too fatiguing; moreover, riding with a straight leg and a long stirrup—which they did, virtually standing as they rode in a high saddle—would make the trot impossible. To rise properly to a trot, you must bend your legs and shorten your stirrups, and you should not, if possible, be carrying forty-odd pounds of iron above your hips. That is why medieval warriors never trotted in armor and why their war-horses were runners.

We have three basic types of horses named for their gait: coursers, amblers, and trotters. The word *courser* seems to have been reserved for war-horses, but amblers and trotters could be rounseys, palfreys, jennets, or hackneys. The rounsey we have discussed. The palfrey was a noble horse by blood and breeding, as valuable sometimes as the destrier but with a gentle, quiet disposition; the palfrey was highly prized as a mount for traveling or hunting, much used by the high and the mighty on ceremonial occasions and in parades. The jennet was a smaller horse, greatly favored by ladies, and seems to have been Spanish in origin—jennet is the English for the French *jenet*, which in turn is French for the Spanish *gineta*. Despite its suitability as a mount for ladies, in Spain this type of horse was used for fighting; in fact, in the fifteenth and early sixteenth centuries light horsemen in Spain were called *ginetours*. The hackney, whether a trotter or an ambler, was much the same then as today, a good horse of no particular distinction. The laboring horse *du genre vilain* was a pack-animal or draught-horse, but until late in the Middle Ages it was rarely a farm-horse, for farm work was done mostly by oxen.

The destrier was ridden only in action. When

traveling, the knight rode a lesser horse according to his means, while his squire led the destrier.

To get a general idea of the horses a typical knight might have had, let's glimpse the story of Jehan de Saintré, one of the most popular French romances of the mid-fifteenth century (de La Sale, Antoine, *Le Petit Jehan de Saintré*, ch. 15). While a page in the service of the queen of France, Jehan received some money from his lady to equip himself as a young noble should:

> And take here in this little purse 160 crowns, the which I give you to buy a fair, spirited and nimble riding-horse, that shall be full lively and brisk whatever it cost you, up to 80 crowns; and another upstanding one for your everyday riding, up to 20 crowns; and another pair, for 30 crowns, to carry your box and a varlet; and that is a hundred and thirty crowns. With the 30 crowns left over, you shall get fair raiment of cloth made, and clothe both yourself and your serving men in your livery when you go riding. And the remnant you shall have for your spending, as long as any remains.

Later in the same romance we learn how he used his mounts when unhorsed at a tournament:

> At the tenth running it happened that they crossed their two lances, and with the great hurtling of their coursers they ran one against the other, in spite of the tilt [which was of scarlet cloth, hung from a cord]; and Sir Enquerrant's

> courser fell and Saintre's broke a shoulder. Then
> Saintré lit down and got upon a rounsey, and so
> to his pavilion to change coursers.

The word courser is used here to denote a jousting
horse, an instance of the imprecise use of words in
the Middle Ages.

Fig. 6. This is how a horse runs. A courser, about 1450

To the men of the Middle Ages, horses were a
source of great pride and affection, for the horse
could signify the status, wealth, and importance of its
owner. A knight who went about with several spare
destriers would be highly regarded by everyone he

met. Many examples of knightly pride regarding horses and horsemanship can be found in Shakespeare's plays—for instance, in Henry V, during the scene describing the night before the battle of Agincourt, when the leaders of the host of France gather in the dauphin's tent and wait restlessly for the morning while the dauphin brags about his horse.

Terms describing gait are almost the only means we have of telling how the medieval knight rode. Contemporary pictures show clearly enough the seat of the armored warrior, the huntsman, the traveler, the lady on her jennet: but the depicted action of the horses in artistic renditions is not convincing. We know in scenes of battles and jousts that the horses are galloping because the artist has drawn them at full stretch, both forelegs out in front and both hind-legs out behind, in an attitude no horse can possibly get itself into. This inaccurate artistic view of the gal-loping horse has lasted, quite curiously, until almost the present time. In the innumerable color prints and paintings of hunting and racing scenes made in the last century, nearly everyone depicts horses running *ventre á terre*. The medieval sculptor and painter too often drew horses' legs going in unison, both near legs going one way together and both off-side ones going the other. Such a rendition does not help deter-mine the actual gait the artist wanted to portray, for a horse's legs actually go one after the other during a gallop (fig. 6).

By the second quarter of the sixteenth century new methods of warfare had come into use, brought about by the increasing use of artillery, and the day of the fully armored knight was over. The military leaders of France, Germany, and Spain sought new cavalry tactics in the face of the vastly increased effectiveness of well-trained infantry, often armed with firearms, and the shattering power of cannon. The French, who had been the originators and chief upholders of the ideals of chivalry, held on stubbornly to the old concept of the charge *en haye*—attack in line–of armored knights with the lance, while the German system was for heavily armored men to charge in column. The weakness of the French method was its tendency to break up in the face of cannon and arquebus fire. In the great wars in Italy during the first half of the sixteenth century, for example, the French *gens d'armes* acquired the uncomplimentary nickname "hares in armor" because they ran away so fast. But the German method had even greater disadvantages: when a column charged upon an adversary, if the ranks did not break at once the whole mass would come to a halt. The front rank would be furiously engaged, while all those behind would be unable to get at the foe at all. They simply sat on their horses and waited. If their enemy had artillery, the dense mass of horsemen provided a sitting target. Fabrizio Colonna, commanding a force of German cavalry that had stood under fire for some time in this fashion, told the Frenchman who captured him that one cannon-ball had knocked over 35 men and horses.

By the middle of the sixteenth century, Germans

had developed new tactics based upon the use of a new weapon. Through the second half of the fifteenth century experiments were made with the handgun, but it required both hands to be managed at all. After about 1535 a small handgun had been perfected, and in the 1540s it came to be known as a pistol. This gun could easily be managed in one hand and the rider could carry three of them–two in holsters in front of his saddle and one in his right boot– giving him three shots before he had to reload. From this use of the weapon developed the troops of pistoleers, armored horsemen carrying three pistols each. The intended use of these pistoleers was for the troop to ride at its adversary, fire its pistols, and then charge home with the sword into the resulting confusion. It was fine in theory, but often hopeless in practice. It is not easy to shoot with a pistol when riding hard (except for a film actor in an American Western), and when the pistol was an early wheellock it was even more difficult. Sometimes you loosed off too soon; sometimes you fired too low and blew off your horse's ears; sometimes–much worse– the men behind you fired too soon and blew your ears off. The only possible way such a maneuver could succeed was by a disciplined holding of your fire until you could see the whites of your enemy's eyes, then letting each of them have it, all together.

This tactic rarely worked, so a new one developed; it was called the caracole. Your troop cantered up to within pistol shot of its opponents; the front rank fired and immediately peeled off to the left and the right to allow the second rank to fire; the second rank did the same in order to let number three have a go, and so on. Meanwhile, of course, enemy cannon were mowing your side down and arquebusiers were thinning you out. Figure 7 shows something of the difficulties of this maneuver. We are looking at the central point of the front rank. The man on the left has fired his shot and is wheeling away to his left, but the second rank man behind him has been shot down; his riderless horse will tangle with the wheeling front-rank man. In the background the front-rank man is about to wheel off to his right, but his horse has been killed, so the man behind him will be put in jeopardy. If the caracole was well carried out, with iron discipline and resolution, it was quite effective. Before the end of the sixteenth century, the "heavy" cavalry (though much lighter than in the 1490s, for only partial armor was worn) had reverted to the steady charge with sword.

Fig. 7. Pistoleers carrying out a caracole movement

Fig. 8. Effigy of Sir Robert de Shurland, in the church at Minster, Isle of Sheppey. About 1320

A Knight and His Horse

In the old church at Minster in the Isle of Sheppey is the once-splendid tomb of a knight of King Edward I's time, Sir Robert de Shurland. He was lord of the manor of Shurland in the parish of Eastchurch and warden of the Cinque Ports. Edward I of England had made de Shurland a knight banneret for distinguished service at the siege of Caerlaverock in Scotland in 1300. Sir Robert's sculptured figure lies in full armor under a stone canopy; the color that once adorned it has faded, dust and closely cut initials mar its surface. Some of those initials were made this century, others more than 300 years ago. But the sculpture remains a remarkable monument. Perhaps the most unusual thing about it is the horse's head carved on the stone slab upon which the effigy rests. The way it is carved suggests that this head rises from water, though at Sir Robert's mailed feet is another armed figure that seems to be leading the horse.

There is a legend about Sir Robert de Shurland and his horse, telling how once in a fit of rage de Shurland caused a priest to be buried alive. It's a pity we don't know what the priest had done, but the story is silent about that. A judicial process was about to be brought against Sir Robert for the priest's death when it happened that the king, going down-river in a ship, passed on a calm day close to the Isle of Sheppey. Sir Robert seized this opportunity, swam his horse out to the ship, and sought the king's pardon. Edward, perhaps remembering Sir Robert's past services and certainly impressed by his bold and perilous swimming feat, granted it. Then de Shurland swam his horse back to the shore. Thus far the story might be true, but now it degenerates into fantasy. As he dismounted from his exhausted horse on the beach, Sir Robert was accosted by a hag, who prophesied that one day his horse would be the death of him. Sir Robert impulsively drew his sword and slew his mount to confound the prophecy. The carcass was left on the shore, where its bones bleached in the wind and rain for many years. One day Sir Robert was walking along the sand with a friend, and they came upon the horse's skeleton. Sir Robert laughed and told his friend of the prophecy, and of how he brought it to nothing. Sir Robert then idly kicked the skull, but a splinter of bone went through his shoe into his foot. The wound mortified and the old knight died of it, so the prophecy came true after all.

If there is any truth in the tale, we can see why an apparently swimming horse appears on the monument. On the other hand, the presence of a swimming horse on the tomb may have given rise to the legend; we may never know exactly where truth ends and fantasy begins, or in what way and to what degree the two coexist here. But there must have been some good reason why the horse was there, for this tomb seems to be the only knightly one with a horse on it. Why de Shurland's and not anyone else's? To be sure, it's surprising more medieval tombs don't reflect how essential a horse was to a knight. Consider that in every European land except England and the Scandinavian countries, the very word for a knight is a horse-word: *chevalier* in French, *cavalière* in Italian, *caballero* in Spanish, and *ritter* in German—all terms deriving from a word for horse. Even as long ago as the Roman Empire, the knightly ranks of society were called *equites*, a word obviously related to the horse word *equine*.

Why did the English use the word *knight*? It's an old Anglo-Saxon word *cniht*, meaning a young man of good family; of course, the word aptly describes the social status of the English *chevalier*. We must remember, as well, that in England before the Norman Conquest at Hastings in 1066, the warrior classes, however noble, never fought on horseback. On the Continent they always did. If you were a noble anywhere else on the Continent (except in Scandinavia), you were a horseman; in England you were not.

Some people tend to think that the fully armored horseman appeared suddenly—and for the first time—in 1066 as a terrible new portent of war on the field of Senlac, site of the Battle of Hastings in southeast England. This belief is incorrect. The fully armored horseman first appeared out of Central Asia as long ago as the first century A.D. During this period a people known as Sarmatians began to move westward into the grasslands of South Russia, where the Scythians dwelled. The Sarmatians and Scythians were of the same race and were superb horsemen, but they rode, armed, and fought differently. The Scythians rode small, swift horses and were bowmen, shooting from the saddle. But the Sarmatians rode heavier animals and fought armored with the lance and long sword, giving them a fighting advantage that enabled them to defeat the Scythians and occupy their land. After living for several generations on these South Russian steppes, the Sarmatians were themselves driven out by migrating hordes of Goths moving southward from the Baltic during the third century. These Goths were of the same race that later produced the Anglo-Saxons and Vikings. The Goths adopted the Sarmatians' method of fighting–and soon became quite good at it. During the fourth century, Goths clashed with the legions of Rome, utterly defeating them at a great battle near Adrianople in Thrace in 376. Victory for the Goths came against a vast army of efficient and highly trained legionaries by using the shock-tactics of medieval chivalry: fierce charges by massed bodies of heavy horsemen. After this battle, Romans themselves took large numbers of Gothic cavalry into their pay as mercenaries. Largely because of this fusion of terrifying new forces with the established armies of the Roman Empire, a new, Goth-inspired method of fighting was carried throughout most of Europe. For instead of staying in the eastern countries they had overrun, Gothic horsemen fought in the Empire's hosts everywhere and soon began to settle and conquer everywhere too. They founded a kingdom in Spain

Fig. 9. Roman Cavalryman, about A.D. 70

that endured for more than 300 years, and in the end they completely overran and occupied the whole of Italy, including Rome herself.

It is not surprising that the Goths' methods of fighting were adopted wherever Rome ruled. After all, successful methods tend to perpetuate. Even the war band of Arthur, the great Romano-British leader who held the Saxon invaders at bay for over fifty years, was armed and mounted in the Gothic manner. That's why Arthur's men beat the Saxons, who were a poorly armed, undisciplined mob that fought on foot.

Though these Saxons were of the same stock as the Goths, they never learned to fight on horseback, largely because the islands occupied by Saxons were cut off from the trends affecting the art of war in Continental Europe. Even though the Saxons had

become efficient fighters by the time of Alfred the
Great, they still fought on foot, unlike their Gothic
predecessors. Since defeating the Britons 400 years
earlier, the Saxons never had to fight horsemen,
never had to adjust to the changes in fighting brought
on by the use of horses in battle: the Saxons' only
enemies were the fearful Vikings of Scandinavia,
who, when on land, fought on foot just as the Saxons
did. The Saxons were thus beaten at Hastings in 1066
not only by Normans, but by tactics and a theory of
battle they had not had to face since circa A.D. 500.

This Saxon fighting legacy should make it clear
why the English used the old Saxon word *cniht* rather
than the Norman-French word *chevalier*. Yet changes,
as we've seen, took place. The victories of horse over
foot, the alteration in war tactics, and the sheer existence of the medieval knight as a military unit–all
depended upon two bits of iron, a couple of straps,
and a buckle or two. Consider the use of stirrups in
the art and science of horsemanship. Try to imagine
that you are on a large, broad horse; you have a saddle, but no stirrups, so you are seated like ancient
Greek and Roman cavalrymen who wore little armor
and used light spears and light swords. Now imagine
that you have a mail shirt weighing perhaps 35
pounds, a mail coif (hood) weighing about four
pounds, and a small nut-shaped helmet weighing
about three pounds. You have a heavy spear about 10
feet long and weighing 10 pounds or so, unlike the
ancient Greeks and Romans. If you tuck the spear's
butt end up under your right arm, level it toward

your left across your horse's neck, and go forward at a fast canter, what happens? You fall off. Now instead of your lance, imagine you have a long sword, with a blade about 30 inches long and weighing 2½ pounds. Pretend you are sitting firmly in your saddle and taking a great full-armed swipe at an imaginary foe out on your right side, about seven feet away. What happens? You fall off again. You see, wearing this sort of armor or using these weapons (which is what the Sarmatians and Goths used) required a warrior to carry a lot of weight (say 50 pounds)—all above the waist. Without support for the feet, such a warrior just could not remain in the saddle. This medieval warrior would have a shield, too, hanging from his neck, so there's another four pounds or so, still above the waist. Now add stirrups to the scene, but let them right out so that the leg is straight, like a cowboy's. You'll see that you don't fall off at all. Knights in a medieval saddle did even better, for it was made to rise in a narrow ridge standing some way clear of the horse's backbone; so with a long stirrup a knight would be virtually standing up. In this way he was properly supported either to take a tremendous blow on the point of his lance or to swing side to side from the hips as he made great sweeps with sword, axe, or mace. If a medieval sword blow found its target, shearing off an opponent's arm or leg, the knight delivering the blow wouldn't ordinarily have been unseated by the shock; if the sword blow missed, the knight still wouldn't fall because his right foot would correct his balance.

Incidentally, as gruesome and unfortunate as it may sound to us in the late twentieth century, sword strokes in medieval times did occasionally cut off people's heads, arms, and legs. It may seem fanciful, and we do read about such things in medieval *chansons de geste*, poems telling of heroic deeds that may be more legendary than real, though no less important and telling. Yet enough carved-up skeletons have been recovered from battlefield grave-pits to indicate that such carnage did occur in the Middle Ages.

Though too heavy to wield on horseback without stirrups, medieval weapons aren't nearly as heavy as many people imagine. Between 1100 and 1500, a typical sword weighed only about 2½ pounds, though a large man might have one weighing as much as four pounds. In the same way a horseman's axe only weighed about 1½ pounds to 2 pounds. Even those great axes the Vikings used on foot only weighed about three pounds. A mace might weigh as much as six pounds, but the average was about four pounds. These figures run counter to the popular belief about weights of medieval weapons, but I own a dozen or so medieval swords, several axes, and a mace, and I've handled and weighed literally hundreds, so I know these weights are correct.

We've drifted from our horse, but not without good reason. It is necessary to realize something about the truth of medieval weapons, about what they were capable of doing, in order to appreciate fully not only the way men wielded them while riding on horseback but also the crucial relationship between knight, weapon, and horse in the art of medieval battle.

Fig. 10. Fully armored man-at-arms, about 1440

Consider an account in the most sober history of the Lombards, a race closely akin to the Goths. Written by Paul the Deacon in the eighth century, it concerns a warrior who ran an opponent through with his lance, lifted him out of his saddle, and held him kicking and struggling on the end of it. The poor fellow was one of the Byzantine *cataphractoi,* armored cavalrymen, so he weighed a good deal. If the feet of the warrior initiating the blow had been dangling from the saddle, he could never have been able to do that to the *cataphractoi.* My point is simply to show that the early use of stirrups was crucial, an important truth overlooked for years by historians and archaeologists. In fact, about thirty-five to forty years ago some publications by eminent historians and archaeologists claimed that the stirrup was unknown before about A.D. 650, but that is definitely not the case. Sculptured figures in India of about 120 B.C. clearly show stirrups (or stirrup-loops, which are the same thing), and it is known that the Sarmatians of the first century A.D. used stirrups. In addition, the known military facts of the battle practice of armored cavalrymen of the first few centuries A.D. supplies any other evidence that may be needed.

The matter of stirrups is not frivolous or trivial; they were the absolute basis, in a literal sense, of the medieval knight's fighting power. The most skillful and most highly regarded act of knightly combat was "spear-play" (*hastiludum*), the running together of two combatants with long lances on powerful horses. It was called jousting. Though I shall have more to say about it in Chapter IV, at this point I want simply to describe the essence of a joust. It called for more skill, both military and equestrian, than any other form of single medieval combat. Though the knight's role was important, the horse made the joust what it was, for the outcome depended as much upon the horse's skill and courage as upon the rider's.

Imagine a knight getting set to joust, or run a course, in the earlier days of chivalry before plate armor, say about 1260. This knight would be armed

Fig. 11. Jousting seat, off side

much like his Gothic predecessor. He is in full mail—
long *chausses* (long stockings) on his legs, a long
hauberk (shirt), and a coif over his head. He wears a
great helm, too, completely enclosing his face and
bearing upon it a crest made of leather or parchment.
His shield covers all of his left side. In his right hand
is a lance; its shaft is about 11 feet long, a plain pole
of ash tapering toward the head, which is made of
finely tempered steel with a two-edged blade about
six inches long. That blade tapers to a socket into
which the shaft is fastened.

When he is ready to go, he lowers this great
spear, tucking the butt end firmly under his arm and
inclining the shaft over his horse's neck pointing over
to the left. In Figures 11 and 12 I have drawn the
knight from both the left and the right side so that
you can see how a knight would "dress" his shield
and hold his lance. In Figure 13 you get a dead-cen-
ter bird's-eye view of how this knight and his opponent would run together. The knight then leans well

Fig. 12. Jousting seat, near side

forward, tucks in his chin, holds his shield well up, and settles firmly into the high "arçon" of his saddle; at the same time he pushes his feet well forward into his stirrups and charges. Our knight can't see much of the other fellow, only the other fellow's helm and shield and horse. The knight must decide in a few seconds where to hit his foe, in the helm or shield? If the helm is hit, it might get torn from the foe's head, but the knight's lance is more likely to glance off; if the knight hits his foe's shield squarely, the foe could be unhorsed. At the last second, the knight takes aim and gives a great thrust forward, rising in his stirrups a bit as he hits his foe. A lot depends on this last rise and thrust. If the knight rises too high (don't forget, the foe is going to hit our knight as well), the knight is liable to sail right over his horse's crupper. But if the thrust added to our knight's speed enables him to hit his foe first, perhaps just a split second sooner, the foe will probably go down instead.

Even if neither knight leaves the saddle, imagine the tremendous impact. Together the two opponents would be moving at about fifty miles an hour, and

Fig. 13. How jousters run together

each knight and horse would weigh as much as a small van. All that speed and all that weight are going to be concentrated in the tiny, sharp points of the lances. In most cases even the stoutest lance would break at impact, but if it didn't break or glance off armor, a knight would be lucky to be simply unhorsed, for otherwise the weapon would probably go right through the knight, armor and all.

Fig. 14. The other fellow

You can see why the knight's horse had to have nerves of steel and a steadfast heart to do this sort of thing. Careful breeding and training went into the various strains of great horse, or destrier, the supreme animal for the joust, trained and bred just for that combat. Why was this horse called "destrier"? The name comes from the Latin dexter, the right-hand side.

The usual explanation for the application of this word to the horse is that, when traveling, the squire led the destrier on the right hand of the knight. Maybe so, but it's an unconvincing reason for the adoption of the word *destrier.* Consider a far more believable theory: as you know, at a canter or a gallop, a horse's forelegs don't move together; one or the other of them leads. When a horse is turning, the leading foreleg has to be on the inside of the curve. If you watch a horse doing a figure eight, you'll notice that, where the curves cross and the horse begins to circle in the reverse direction, he will change his step in order to lead with the other foreleg. If he didn't he'd probably cross his legs and fall. Now, when a horse is running in a joust, he must never swerve to the left, inward toward the opposing horse. On the other hand he must always be ready in a split second to swerve away to the right. So he must run always leading with the right foreleg. A horse left to itself will generally tend always to lead with the same leg, it doesn't matter which, but a jousting horse must be trained to lead with the right: hence the name *destrier*, a derivation from the Latin for right-hand side. It does seem probable that at some time a chronicler, not being a practical horseman, misread a Latin phrase describing why a dextrarius was so called, assuming that it meant the horse "is led on the right" instead of "leads with the right," an expression meaningless to a non-horseman. (I owe this theory based on practical horsemanship to my friend Mr. E. Holmes.)

Saddle, Bridle, and Horse Armor

The word *harness* used to mean equipment and applied to the body-armor of a soldier. Today it is generally taken to mean the equipment of work horses such as vanners or coach-horses. For the riding-horse we speak of saddle and bridle, or simply "tack." Bridles have hardly changed since ancient times; the kinds of bridles used in the Middle Ages were the same in principle as those of the Roman Empire and of the Victorians. The saddle, on the other hand, has changed a good deal. The ancients did not use it at all, and a medieval saddle was different from a modern one. Before we consider horse armor, which was always rare, we must look at the essential tack that every horse had to have.

The bridle consists of the headstall, the bit, and the reins. The headstall is a series of straps fitting onto the horse's head to keep the bit in place. The headpiece passes across the head behind the ears, while the headband goes across in front of the ears. The throat lash is a downward continuation of the headband that goes under the horse's jaw, preventing

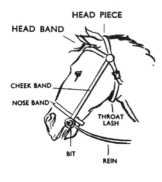

Fig. 15. Headstall

him from pulling his bridle off. From the points at each side of the head where these three straps meet two long straps, called the cheek bands, pass along the animal's cheeks. The lower ends of the bands are fastened to the bit. The noseband goes across the face between the nostrils and the eyes. The diagram in Figure 15 shows how these straps were arranged.

Bits used in the Middle Ages were like modern ones—the bridoon, the snaffle, and the curb. (Figure 16 provides a glimpse of what these types look like.) One common bit, however, is rather confusing, for in medieval pictures it looks like a curb bit, but in fact it is not. It is an ordinary snaffle with the lower cheek bar elongated downward and outward. The curb, though known in ancient times (Xenophon mentions it), generally was not used in the Middle Ages until after about 1350. One way these bits differed from modern ones was that the extremity of the bit, where it stuck out of the side of the horse's mouth, was usually covered by an ornamental boss.

What I have tried to describe is a complete headstall, but often parts of it were left out. We often find pictures showing horses without noseband or headpiece, quite often without a throat latch as well. One piece of comparatively modern tack that seems not to have been used until late in the sixteenth century is the martingale, a long strap fastened at one end to the headstall, passing down between the forelegs and having its other end attached to the girth. The idea is to prevent the horse from throwing up his head and clouting his rider on the nose.

Until about 1275 only a single pair of reins was used, but later it was more common to have a double pair. As a rule one of these was a narrow strap, the other a broad one. Generally we find that the broad rein was fastened directly to the boss of the bit, while the narrow one was attached to the end of the branch, if a branched snaffle or a curb was used. With an ordinary snaffle or a bridoon, both reins were fixed to the bit itself. The broad reins were often adorned with those wide bands of stuff we so often see in pictures, their lower edges variously cut into fantastic shapes and their sides embellished with embroidery or with applied metal decorations. These

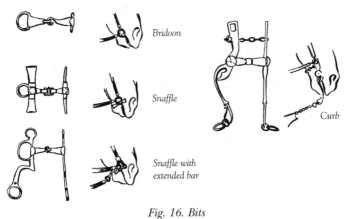

Bridoon

Snaffle

Snaffle with extended bar

Curb

Fig. 16. Bits

39

arrangements, of course, often varied. Both pairs of reins might be of the same breadth, or the broad one might be fastened to the end of the branch and the narrow one to the bit instead of the other way around. It all seems to have been a matter of personal taste. The broad reins were seldom attached directly to the bit or the branch; a short length of chain was fastened to it, between six and ten inches long, and the end of the rein was fixed to this chain.

Though the nomadic horse-breeding Scythians and Sarmatians used saddles, the Ancient Greeks never did. Neither did the Romans, until about A.D. 300. Generally the Greeks rode bareback, though sometimes they sat on a cloth on top of the horse. The Roman cavalryman nearly always had a cloth or a sheepskin. The Romans' use of the saddle seems to have occurred when, as I mentioned earlier, they became acquainted with the Gothic heavy cavalry. These early Roman saddles were similar to the first medieval ones, which we can see in many manuscript paintings and in the Bayeux Tapestry, which depicts events leading up to the Norman Conquest of England in 1066.

During the thirteenth century the high-peaked pommel of the war saddle broadened into a wide front plate (called the burr-plate) that protected the rider from the waist almost to the knees. At the same time the cantle at the back spread forward to embrace the rider's hips (see Figures 11 & 12). This kind of saddle is believed to have been introduced into Western Europe through contacts made during

Fig. 17. Hanry V's war-saddle.
Westminster Abbey

Fig. 18. Saddle of the Emperor
Frederic III. Made in 1477 by
Lorenz Colman of Augsburg.
Kunsthistorisches Museum, Vienna

the Crusades by the chivalry of the West with the Arabs, who always used this sort of saddle.

A few examples of these early saddles survive. The Royal Armory of Spain at Madrid contains an early saddle that is listed in an old inventory as belonging to King Jaime I of Aragon (1213-76). The English have the saddle of Henry V (1413-22), which hangs above his tomb in Westminster Abbey. It is now a tattered and sad-looking relic, a result of the wearing away of its covering of blue velvet powdered with fleurs-de-lis. But since only the bare bones are left, we can still see clearly how it was made (Figure 17).

A medieval saddle consists of the wooden framework, called the arçon or saddletree, and the seat, the metal fittings, the straps, and the covering. The tree is of various parts, generally made of beech-wood: the "bands" or plates, two flat boards that sit one on either side of the horse's backbone, are joined together by the arch of the burr-plate in front and the arch of the cantle behind. Above the bands and between the arched pieces is the seat, while the girth-straps

41

and the fittings for the stirrup-leathers are fixed to the bands below the seat. Henry V's saddle (Figure 17) shows this construction clearly. You can see how high the seat is above the bands—about five inches clear of the horse's backbone. You can see too its original padding made of hay.

The statutes drawn up in 1403 to regulate the work of the saddlers of Limoges have survived, providing us with some useful information about the actual making of saddles. These statutes stipulate that the joints of the arçon must be well stuck with glue and reinforced with iron rivets, and that the arçon should be "well sinewed above and below and that the underneath should be well-covered so that the horse's sweat shall not damage the sinews." The whole of the tree, inside and out, was covered with a close web of fibers made by the fine shredding of ox-sinews. Good hot glue was then used to keep everything together. When it was cold and dry, more glue was applied, and the tree was covered with linen. Then the metal parts were fitted, and the saddle was turned over to the *garnisseurs*, who covered the inside with sheepskin and the outside with velvet or leather (calfskin or the fine leather of Cordova).

Later in the fifteenth century the "arms" of the cantle became more slender, as you can see in Figure 18, which shows a saddle made in 1477 for the Emperor Frederic III (1453-1509). Later on it became even smaller and was supported on either side by a slender bar, while the burr-plate broadened considerably (Figure 19).

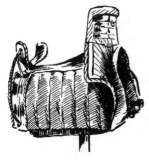

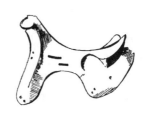

Fig. 19. War-saddle of about 1520.
Wallace Collection, London

Fig. 20. Riding saddle, c. 1450

In the drawing of Henry V's saddle you can see a couple of staples with pierced heads in the part of the bands of the saddle-tree that project forward over the horse's withers in front of the burr-plate. These are for the attachment of the breast-strap, a broad band across the horse's chest that prevents the saddle from slipping back. Similarly a single staple behind the cantle is on each side to take the crupper, a band that goes around the animal's buttocks to prevent the saddle from slipping forward. These bands were often decorated with elaborately dagged edges and with embroidered designs or little metal ornaments. These were often in the form of shields, made of copper-gilt with the arms of the owner in colored enamels, and sometimes were disc-shaped with an enameled design—usually armorial. I have drawn horses wearing this sort of ornament in Figure 4, but often the girth alone was relied upon to keep the saddle secure as in Figure 3.

That, very briefly, was the war saddle. For hunting or traveling, saddles were made in the same manner and of the same materials, but the shapes differed from the war saddle. Many hunting and traveling saddles survive, all dating from between about 1380 and 1480, and these rich, valuable pieces offer a rare glimpse into the fine craftsmanship of the period, for their wooden "trees" are covered with beautifully carved and painted ivory. None of their more humdrum poor relations, the ones simply covered with leather, have survived. But the lovely parade saddles show us clearly enough the form of the everyday saddle. In form they revert to the old pre-Crusading war saddles, having a high-peaked pommel and a fairly low, but adequately supporting, cantle (Fig. 20).

In principle, medieval stirrups were exactly like their modern counterparts, though there were a few variations in form. It is possible to trace a clear progression of stirrup-types from about A.D. 700 onward, but for our purposes it will be enough to glance at the types likely to have been used by our knight.

Up to about 1350, the most usual form of stirrup looked triangular (Fig. 21). But during the second half of the fourteenth century, lopsided stirrups curiously came into use. The idea, I suppose, was to prevent the inside of the stirrup from digging into the horse by accident during combat. Another type of stirrup that developed about this time had broad sides, tapering toward the toe. This design was sensible, for it prevented the foot from "riding home" in the stirrup, especially when the foot was stretched forward, far out, in jousting—that is, getting pushed right into

Fig. 21. Stirrups, 1000-1500

Left, about 1000; center, about 1260; right, about 1350

Left, about 1350, center, about 1380; right, about 1450

About 1500

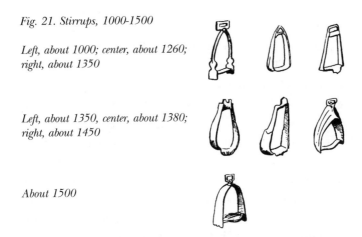

the stirrup until it came against the ankle bones. If a knight were unhorsed while his feet were well-set in the stirrups, far up, he could have gotten dragged along because his foot wouldn't come out. Not until the end of the fifteenth century were stirrups rounded across the top.

Sometimes you may notice in a medieval picture that a horse—not necessarily a war-horse—seems to have studs on its shoes like the studs on soccer cleats. In medieval times large-headed nails often were used to secure the horse's shoe. Even chariot-horses of the Celts had the same kinds of nails.

Armor for the medieval horse developed along the same lines as man's armor. But the early forms of fabric, leather, and mail for the horse never entirely gave way to plate. Though splendid bards of plate-armor were built in the fifteenth and sixteenth centuries, these were only for the horses of great and wealthy men. The horse armor of the ordinary knight continued to be made of the older, lighter, and less costly materials.

Though known to have been used to some extent on chariot horses of ancient times, horse armor never fully developed until warriors began to fight as heavy cavalry. The first warriors to incorporate this cavalry approach, as we have seen, were the Sarmatians, but it was the Goths who introduced the tactics, fighting methods, and armor of the knight to the Middle Ages. In the history of the mid-sixth-century Gothic wars, written by Procopius, secretary to the great Byzantine general Belisarius, we read how the Gothic king Witiges marched against Rome: he did it by leading a great army of horse and foot, "and most of them, as well as their horses, were clad in armor."

We then hear no more about horse armor until about 1150, six centuries later. While it may seem that such armor went out of fashion, we should not assume that it was never worn during that time. Nevertheless, no historian or chronicler—or, more important, no poet—mentions it for 600 years, which does seem to suggest that it was at least rare.

After the middle of the twelfth century, more references to horse armor appear, but most are literary. A few pictures show horses with bards of mail but many more show horses with flowing caparisons (another name for bard, though caparison is used more to define rich and colorful trappings of fabric; bard more properly indicates some sort of armor.

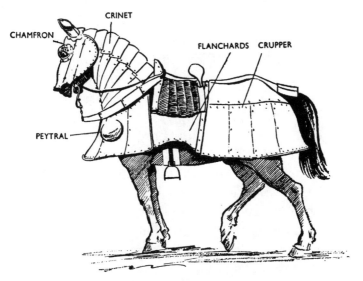

Fig. 22. Diagram showing complete horse-armor, style of about 1510

However, with the usual semantic inconsistency of the medieval period, both words are used interchangeably). Bards of mail appear so rarely that we must assume that they were never very popular. Of course, we can't tell what may have been beneath the fabric caparisons. It seems unlikely that full bards of mail were used often, for so large an amount of mail would have been unbearably heavy. But pieces of plate armor or of leather for the head are often shown as early as 1250.

Interesting English records of late thirteenth-century horse armor, as well as accounts of the army status of the warrior whose horse was "covered," survive from the Exchequer accounts of 1297 and 1298. They provide complete payrolls in which the value of every horse is entered, together with the rider's name. The one for 1298 gives the total of cavalry in the pay of the king (Edward I) for one of his campaigns against the Scots. Some of these paid cavalrymen were knights, but most were ordinary troopers. In the Middle Ages troopers generally were called sergeants, though the nobly born trooper was called a squire or valet.

To understand the world of knights, it is necessary to have some idea of the stratification within medieval society and within armies. In England, a young nobleman aspiring to knighthood had to do his military service among the rank and file, taking the pay of a shilling a day just like everyone else, and doing the same service. Some of the most famous war leaders of the fourteenth century started in this way; in fact, two famous names appear in the roll of 1298, John de Argentine and Reginald Cobham, both serving in the retinue of Hugh le Despencer. Thirty years later both were among the most renowned commanders in the armies of Edward III and the Black Prince of Wales. When that redoubtable prince was a boy, Reginald Cobham was in charge of him as a sort of military tutor and "shoulder-companion," to use an apt Anglo-Saxon expression. Sir Reginald Cobham lived to a good old age, dying in 1361 of plague. He has a most splendid monument over his tomb in the church of Lingfield in Surrey.

Young Reginald drew his shilling a day as an ordinary trooper. Keep in mind: there were different grades of trooper, and only those who had "covered" horses qualified for a shilling. An uncovered horse rated only sixpence or eightpence a day for his rider.

In an Exchequer entry of 1277, we find that sixteen shillings were paid for two coverings of linen for two of the king's horses. This linen was to be put "under the iron covering" to prevent its galling the horse. This "iron" might have been mail, but references in an inventory only a few years later indicate it might have been plate. This inventory of the armor and weapons left by Raoul de Nesle, constable of France who fell in the battle of Courtrai in 1302, lists the use of solid defenses for the flanks and crupper. A later inventory (of Guillaume de Hainault, 1358) includes "2 pairs of covers of iron of mail and 2 pairs of covers of iron of plates." So the "iron" of the king's bards in the 1277 entry might have been of mail, of large plates, or of small plates riveted to the inside of a textile bard in the same way that a "coat of plates" was made for a man.

One thing to note about these horse armors: all three were made for the use of great and wealthy men. Horses of ordinary knights and sergeants probably had leather or fabric bards, much lighter and less costly yet on the whole probably just as effective. The same applies to men's armor, as well; all through the Middle Ages it seems that only a minority of cavalrymen wore complete armor. We must remember that the brasses and sculptured monuments we often see show the figures of men of high rank. Troopers are not shown, and their equipment on the whole was lighter, to match their lighter horses (and lighter purses, too).

By the end of the fourteenth century the bard of plate as we know it had fully developed, though none from that early date actually survive. There are a few odd pieces, mostly chanfrons, which date from the early years of the fifteenth century, but the earliest complete bard is of about 1450-60. It is an Italian armor (indeed the only Italian horse armor of the fifteenth century) and bears a Milanese armorer's mark and the name INOSENS.

Only six complete bards of the period before 1500 survive. Except for chanfrons, they are rarely shown in German painting and sculpture before about 1510, and never in Italian paintings. Considering how rare they must have been, we are lucky to have six left. Of the six, four are especially fine and one is absolutely superb. The sixth is in good shape but incomplete.

The most important of these bards is in the Waffensammlung in Vienna. It was made in 1477 by Augsburg armorer Lorenz Helmschmied for Emperor Frederic III, and survives in almost perfect condition. The bard is complete, even to the saddle, and is rich in elaborate decoration of blue and gold, with the double eagle of the empire embossed on the main pieces. This armor is not only rich and splendid, but also a superb work of art. The remaining five "Gothic" bards are not as lavishly decorated, but are none the worse for that. We would be justified in considering the emperor's rich bard a ceremonial armor,

Fig. 23. Barded horses, about 1420. The one on the left has a fabric bard, emblazoned with the rider's arms, while the horse on the right has a chanfron of plate, with a partial crinet of plate worn over mail, and the breastband is covered with mail

but the others were "field" armor, for use in battle, not a parade. The two best of these are in England. In the armories at the Tower of London is a bard that, until 1926, was in the possession of the great German family of Anhalt. It was made at some time about 1480, probably for Waldemar VI, duke of Anhalt-Zerbst, who reigned over his principality from 1473 to 1508. This bard shows the typical German style, the so-called "Gothic," with its cusped edges and elegantly fluted surfaces. The central plate of the peytral is decorated with an embossed grotesque head, part human and part lion. Each plate of the crinet is embossed, and the crupper's two side pieces are joined along the line of the horse's backbone with a humorous monster made of jointed and embossed steel, whose head covers the top of the horse's tail.

The saddle does not belong to the bard, and the small flanking plates under the saddle are missing.

This Anhalt armor seems by its style to have been built in the same workshop as the one in the Wallace Collection in London. This belonged to the Freiherr Pancraz von Freyburg, a baron of Austria in whose castle of Hohenaschau the armor was preserved until 1857. Though not as rich as the Anhalt armor, this bard I believe has greater beauty of line (maybe because it is simpler). Its outstanding impressiveness nevertheless seems related to two conditions: it is superbly mounted and set up, and the armor for the rider who bestrides it was made at the same time by the same armorer for the same baron, Pancraz von Freyburg. My drawing in Figure 24 gives an impression of the general look of this splendid armor. No other armor anywhere, I believe, coincides so perfectly with our romantic ideas about a knight, yet there is nothing bogus about this armor. A few slight restorations have been done here and there, but they only repair or replace bits that were worn out or lost.

If you have not been to the Wallace Collection to see this armor, it is worth a special visit. You will not regret it; nor, I think, will you ever forget it. It stands free in the middle of one of the rooms, not obscured by a glass case or hedged about with barriers. You can get right up to it, walk right around it, and look at it from every angle. You could touch it, but an attendant will no doubt stop you. That's not because he or she doesn't want you to admire and

Fig. 24. Armor for man and horse, once belonging to the Freiherr Pancraz von Freyburg, made about 1475 in Landshut. Wallace collection, London. Only the saddle doesn't belong to this otherwise complete harness; it is somewhat later in date, about 1520

appreciate it as much as possible, but because your fingers will leave prints on the surface of the metal. Despite the grease it is covered with, in a few hours the armor you dabbed would be decorated with a fine set of your fingerprints in rust. So don't touch it; if you want to look closely, or see one bit hidden behind another, ask an attendant and he or she will no doubt be happy to show you. But do go and see the Freiherr Pancraz.

An armor similar to the Anhalt and Freyburg armors is in the Musee de l'Armee in Paris. This piece came from the Arsenal at Strasbourg and is like the other two except that it still has its flanchards under the saddle, and the crupper extends around the back of the horse's hindquarters. The fifth extant bard, still of German fashion, is in the Museo Stibbert in Florence, Italy. The peytral is missing, as well as the flanchards, and the style of the fluted decoration on the crupper is far from elegant; in fact, it is ugly. The last surviving fifteenth-century bard, in the Civic Museum in Vienna, is important because it is considerably earlier than the others and is the only Italian bard in existence.

Unfortunately the most complete horse armor ever made no longer exists. It was made by Lorenz Helmschmied of Augsburg in 1480-81 for the Archduke (later Emperor) Maximilian, and had complete leg armor as well, right down to the fetlocks. We know what it looked like because it appears in two paintings now in the Waffensammlung in Vienna.

At about this time armor was also made for dogs,

probably to protect them when hunting boar. An example of dog armor is in the Royal Armory at Madrid, but such armor must have been rare.

Many chroniclers of the period 1450-1520 write of armies in which hundreds of cavalry rode on barded horses, but in most cases they are referring to material of textile or of leather. An entry in an inventory of Charles VI of France in 1411 includes an armor for man and horse made of Syrian leather, and in the Carolino-Augustinum Museum at Salzburg there is a leather horse armor of 1525. The Tower of London has a pair of leather cruppers of Henry VIII's time, the only survivors of the total of sixty-one that appear in the inventory of 1561.

By the sixteenth century complete bards of plate seem to have become more common; certainly a considerable number from that century survive, most of the finest, most elaborate workmanship. Like armors for men, the character of horse armor changed after about 1500. Gone were the slender lines, the cusped edges and elegant fluting. Instead the whole appearance became more burly and the armor itself more enveloping (figure 22).

One of the finest bards of the early sixteenth century sits in the Tower of London. Like the armor of Pancraz von Freyburg, this piece is part of a complete armor for man and horse. It was probably made in London in 1511 by one of the Italian armorers imported by Henry VIII. When it was new it must have presented an unforgettable appearance, for its entire surface, in every piece of both armors, was decorated with engraving. The whole thing was originally covered with silver-gilt. We can look at it and admire its fine form and the artistry of its decoration, but it takes a concerted effort of imagination to picture it as it was with the magnificently handsome young king wearing it, both he and his mount gleaming all over with gold.

The Tournament

It is difficult to think of a knight's horse without thinking of jousts and tournaments. In fact, we probably think more often of knights engaging in tournaments than of fighting in battles, and we are right to do so, for this chivalric sport played an important part in the life of the ruling classes of medieval Europe. That might suggest that only the ruling classes were interested in tournaments, which was not so. In the Middle Ages tournaments claimed the attention of average people similarly to the way events for race horses and jockeys do today, as well as for baseball and football games—indeed, any sporting event where the many who don't participate gather to admire the skill and courage of the few who do. Even though a person surely had to be of knightly rank to take part in a medieval tournament, the humblest artisan or peasant took pleasure in watching and took pride in being able to appreciate the skilled form shown by the contestants.

Keep in mind what is meant by the phrase "of knightly rank." In the first place, it refers to persons "of gentle birth," an indication that one came from a family that held land and had the right to "bear arms," meaning to display as a personal sign a specific heraldic device or pattern. These "arms" were a bit like family trademarks. Once granted the right to a device, a family had the sole, exclusive right to that device: it could be used by no other family. Basically, the right to bear arms was given only to those who held land and owed "knight service" (military service) to an overlord, and through the overlord to the monarch. Even so, cases did occur where ordinary men—whose parents were townsmen, peasants, or possibly even serfs—were ennobled for performing some outstanding deed or service. True, this type of ennoblement was rare, but it was nevertheless possible. Napoleon's famous remark that every common soldier carried a marshal's baton in his knapsack was nearly as true in 1300 as in 1800.

Outstanding valor—or more often and more important, outstanding skill—found its reward on the field of war or in the tournament. Though difficult and in need of careful tact and even some deception, it was possible for a poor, not propertied soldier to take part in tournaments, provided he had horse and weaponry. In this way he could bring himself to the notice of greater men who would perhaps be glad of his service. But such a soldier, like others, had to be very talented and well-skilled, for the tournament was not only an intensely competitive sport: it was a tough and selective battle school as well. Great barons and war leaders would watch the contestants perform and bestow patronage and protection (house and home too, in some cases) upon those who caught their eye.

In its earlier forms in the age of chivalry, the tournament was a realistic encounter between warriors armed with the weapons of war. But in its decline after the Renaissance, the tournament became a mere pageant for the display of wealth and the symbols of status and power, the men taking part covering themselves with specially designed armor and taking considerable precautions not to get hurt. But in all its forms, whether involving real fighting or skillful display, the intention was never to hurt any horse in a tournament. From the beginning it was a foul of the dirtiest kind to strike your opponent's horse. Ordinances or rules drawn up in the late fifteenth century by John Tiptoft, earl of Worcester, really were an up-to-date English version of the many rules written far earlier. Tiptoft's rules say, in part: "He who strykythe an Horse schal have noo prize." No matter how well you might perform in a tournament, striking a horse led to disqualification.

In the age of chivalry, the sport of the tournament functioned as the school of the true knight and those aspiring to knighthood. A *chanson de geste* composed by Girard de Rousillon, a knight of the thirteenth century, speaks of the pride of a *chevalier* of France who can say of his forbears, "Not one of us has had for a father a knight who died in house or home. All have died in battle of cold steel." If I were writing here strictly about chivalry, not just about its outward trappings and appearances, it would be necessary to say much about the splendid ideals it embodied, by no means all warlike. But for the scope of this text, suffice it simply to quote and comment upon two fragments from medieval writers. The English chronicler Roger of Hoveden wrote in the twelfth century: "A youth must have seen his blood flow and felt his teeth crack under the blow of his adversary and have been thrown to the ground twenty times. Thus will he be able to face real war with the hope of victory." One acceptable extrapolation of that quote is the suggestion that, in the medieval mindset, receiving such adversarial blows and seeing such blood enabled a knight-bound youth to face real life with the hope of success. About 200 years later, the great English poet Geoffrey Chaucer, writing in the General Prologue to *The Canterbury Tales*, described the "Squier" in this way:

> Wel coude he sitte on hors, and faire ride;
> He coude songes make, and wel endite,
> Juste and eek daunce, and wel portraye and write.
> ....
> ....
> Curteis he was, lowely and servisable,
> And carf beforn his fader at the table.

Though Chaucer was a master of gentle satire, we can take him here literally: The ideal knight was not just a tough fighter, forever running about with sword or axe, but a polite, useful, and capable mem-

ber of society. To be a true knight a young man had
to pass tough tests, perhaps similar to those a modern
American might face in attempting to become an
Eagle Scout, but the medieval tests were surely harder, more exacting, and socially exclusive. Of course,
to the medieval test must be added all the warlike
attainments that are no longer required in what was
once called high society. It is important to remember
that knights also had to do many useful things. As
Chaucer tells us, an aspirant to knighthood needed
not only to ride and joust well, but also to dance well.
Chaucer's "Squier" also could compose songs and
verse and, in the lines omitted above, we are told this
particular "Squier" was a lover of some renown. Most
people are not familiar with the idea that the knight
had to write well. But I don't believe, when we read
in the General Prologue that the "Squier" could "wel
portraye and write," that Chaucer is referring to the
ability to create vivid portraits. He probably means
the "Squier" could form his letters well and write with
sense. Every squire had to be courteous, for, as
Chaucer reminds us in his description of the Knight
in *The Canterbury Tales*, courtesy, honor, generosity,
and truth were the foundations of chivalry and of
polite society. In the Middle Ages, the word *courteous*
meant far more than it does today, covering every
dimension of gracious living and proper behavior.
"Lowely and servisable" means the knightly person
must be modest, quiet, well-mannered, tactful, and
soft-spoken to all, and be competent to perform all
sorts of jobs, some purely domestic. Serving at table–

Fig. 25. A mêlée at a

...urnament in about 1170

to "carf beforn his fader"–was one of the most important duties of a page and squire: when a page was
promoted to carve meat at the table, he was really
getting on.

From the age of seven, when a well-born boy
was taken from the care of his mother and her
women, he was trained to do knightly things. But one
notion was especially drummed into him: he had to
do service to others, no matter how messy, lowly, irk-
some, or dangerous it might be. That service was the
knight's *raison d'être*, the mainspring of his life. At
seven years old, a knight-to-be also began to train to
fight. That set in motion the attainment of experience
that led to great skill, the reason medieval warriors
were able to do things in their armor and with their
weapons that seem impossible, almost unimaginable,
to the modern mindset. For instance, a squire or
aspiring knight who could not, with all his armor on,
vault from the ground into his saddle without touching the stirrup would be considered "grade B," far
from prime material.

In the twelfth and thirteenth centuries, tournaments for some warriors were a way of life. Consider
the knights-errant, the poor landless knights. They
were either younger sons who had no part in their
father's estates or professional warriors who had won
no fief of their own to settle down in and live on; or
they were men who had in some way lost or forfeit-
ed or been dispossessed of what they had. For these
knights-errant, tournaments were a way of getting a
living. A knight-errant wasn't necessarily a high-

minded romantic soul who went about the world righting wrongs. Some were that way, of course, but most were tough, hard-bitten professional fighters to whom the tournament was a means to a monetary end. You see, if a knight unhorsed, disarmed, and captured an opponent, he became heir to that foe's horse, arms, and armor from the moment of capture. By the conventions of the laws of chivalry, the defeated foe was compelled to pay, according to his means, a ransom to secure his release. So if a knight were good at tournaments, he could do very well indeed: He would be able to sell the horses and arms he secured, often right on the spot and often right back to the original owner. The ransom money you were going to get was useful security for credit. So the knight-errant wandered (errant means *wandering*) from tournament to tournament, and since there was always one going on somewhere he was rarely out of a job.

England can perhaps lay claim to the two most famous knights-errant of the twelfth century. One was that curious monarch Henry, eldest son of Henry II of England and brother to Richard the Lionhearted and to John. In his father's lifetime this curious Henry was crowned king of England: the father, the "old king," had his hands full ruling over not only England but also two-thirds of France. But the son, this curious Henry, never was given any work to do because, in actuality, his father went on ruling just the same. Our curious Henry also never seemed to have enough money. True enough, he was allowed a great deal of money, but he was such a pleasant, gleeful, and popular young man that he always spent far more than his father allowed him. The son had great leadership ability, it seems, and would probably have ruled well if his father had let him. Partly to pay off his debts, partly to have something to do, he became a "king-errant" and wandered all over Europe with a band of friends, supporters, and hangers-on, taking part in tournaments. Unfortunately, though charismatic, he was not very good at performing in tournaments, and he often caused his friends and his hosts—and probably his adversaries—a good deal of embarrassment. It would be awkward to unhorse or injure the king of England, and the possibility of having to reconcile ransom and protocol must have been a headache.

Ransoms, by the way, were more or less regulated on a fixed scale of charges—a squire was worth so much, a knight a little more, and so on, with princes and kings obviously being at the top of the scale. This scale also was used for noble prisoners taken in war. Though England's ineffectual "young king" Henry was more a source of embarrassment than pride, the country's second twelfth-century knight-errant was just the opposite. He was William Marshal, whose career started at the age of 8 when he was a hostage in the hands of King Stephen. Marshal's career culminated as regent of England when he was 70 years old.

King Stephen (a bad king, but a most charming, accomplished man and a gallant knight) had taken a fancy to his small hostage, and took him into his service. Through courtesy and skill in arms, William soon began to make a name and a good living for himself. He went from tournament to tournament and invariably did well in them, outshining in generosity and outfighting all others. He soon became extremely popular with all types and ranks of men. Though not propertied, he was known and respected by princes and prelates from one end of Europe to the other. Humble men loved him for his unfailing courtesy and generosity toward them, and the proudest and highest-ranked sought his company, advice, and service—whenever it could be given without infringement of William Marshal's feudal obligations to his lord, King Henry II.

Marshal was the most skillful jouster, the most gleeful companion, the wisest counselor, the most loyal vassal—in short, the very embodiment of the ideals of chivalry. He was also the tutor, in military matters, of young King Henry. When Henry was a charming but erratic prince—just a boy—William Marshal took charge of the prince's household. Marshal remained with Henry and got him out of many scrapes until the end of Henry's short life. Marshal's talents were so renown that he became regent of England upon King John's death in 1217, and guardian of John's infant son Henry III.

We know a great deal about the remarkable William Marshal because a long *chanson*, a rhyming chronicle of his achievements, was made after his death by one of his followers, Gerard d'Erlée, who seems to have been with Marshal for most of his many adventures.

The origins of the tournament as a war game are remote and obscure. The Romans had a similar sort of mounted exercise that they called Ludus Troiae (Troy Game), and all the Celtic and Teutonic folk as far back (we may believe) as about 500 B.C. had similar games—as did, of course, the peoples of the ancient world. But the tournament seems to have been first formalized in the way we know it late in the eleventh century, though there is some evidence that something similar to the French tournament took place in Germany as early as 842. This German tournament was organized on a regular basis by Emperor Henry the Fowler (876-936), who set up a commission to inquire into these games and to draw up spear-game laws. But the Conflictus Gallicus or Bataille Français as we know it was essentially a French product. A baron of Anjou, one Geoffrey de Previlly, is credited with its invention (Hic Gaufridus de Preuliaco torneamenta invenit. See Chronichon Turonense, sub anno 1062: Bouquet, *Recuiel de Histoires des Gaulles*, Xll, p. 462).

In its early forms the tournament was simply a friendly battle fought without strategy at a fixed time and place between invited contestants. A baron would announce that a tournament was being held at such and such a place and issue a general invitation to all-comers. When the participants arrived, sides were picked on a simple basis: all who came from the West or the South, say, would oppose all who came from the East or North. The fight would then begin all over the landscape; this mêlée soon resolved itself into a series of single combats, though the code of chivalry allowed a knight, if he got rid of his antagonist, to go to the aid of anyone else on his side. Often two or three knights would assail one combatant, which was not considered in any way unsportsmanlike.

When a fighter was hurt or tired, he could rest for a while. It is believed the word that later on was applied to the place where tournaments were held, the *lists*, originally referred to a series of pens built of hurdles and laid out near the tournament area and into which tired contestants could go to rest. It was a place where, by the rules of combat, they would be safe from attack. When they felt better they could come out and join again in the mêlée.

By the middle of the thirteenth century tournaments had become far more formal and highly organized. The list now was a field, usually near a castle or a town, leveled and cleared of scrub and kept specifically for holding tournaments. At this time, the individual single combat called the joust began to take its place as a regular feature of a tournament. The first day of a tournament perhaps would be given up to these jousts, both on horseback and on foot, while a later day was devoted to the mêlée, the mock battle of two teams opposing each other. The whole thing, which might last a week, would end with a sort of general fête.

An account of a tournament held in 1285 at

Chauvency in France provides telling details. They are contained in a *chanson* written by a *trouvère* named Jacques de Bretac, whose patron was Sire Henri de Blamont, one of the combatants. De Bretac tells of the "Queen of the Tournament" who paid him for his song and of the minstrelsy and dancing that went on in the evenings. The first day was for a general assembly and meeting of the combatants, the second for practice at jousting and what would appear to have been preliminary heats, probably to assess the form of the jousters and to ensure that they were properly matched. The third day was for the jousts themselves. Then there was a rest day, when sides were picked for the mêlée that took place on the fifth day. The last day was for celebration—music, dancing, and general jollity.

The actual combatants were not the only ones who came to these tournaments. Since fighting was confined to a definite area, plenty of scope remained for spectators and, like modern horse races, tournaments always attracted a horde of what we might call unseemly personalities. Though the medieval Fair was a serious commercial function, like modern trade fairs, tournaments reflected much of the spirit of our modern village-green fairs: similar types of entertainment were to be found at tournaments. But one reason governments all over Europe tried hard to prohibit tournaments is that they brought together not simply large numbers of skilled fighting men but also many undesirable and rascally characters. It was all too easy for disaffection or actual rebellion to get off to a good—or rather evil—start at a tournament. The Church was always especially opposed to tournaments, partly for political reasons but more so for moral reasons: A man killed in a tourney was considered to have committed suicide, a highly mortal sin. He was also considered to be risking his livelihood and his family's well-being, putting his tenants (if he had any) in jeopardy, and wasting his time on frivolity—an ecclesiastical attitude similar to some strict churches today decrying the evils of betting and gambling. In medieval times, all the efforts of State and Church to stop tournaments ultimately proved fruitless.

Excommunication was threatened by the Church and sometimes put into effect, but governments took the line adopted by many governments before and since—if you can't stop them, tax them. Governments sought to make money out of tournaments by issuing licenses. If a tournament were held without a license, then heavy fines were imposed.

The occasions upon which tournaments might be called were many: to celebrate the return of a baron from a crusade or a campaign overseas, the marriage of an important personage or a political alliance, the birth of a baby or announcement of a betrothal—nearly any reason would serve. When, for instance, in 1215 the barons of England were assembled at Runnymede to force King John to sign the Great Charter, they found that, once the king had signed and departed, a goodly gathering of knights were present. So a tournament was held in a meadow

Fig. 26. Jousting at a

ournament in about 1420

beside the Thames River. Sometimes a tournament was organized around a judicial trial by combat; once the defendant (or his champion) had fought his duel with the plaintiff (or his champion), the fun could begin.

It is easy for the modern student of medieval life to become confused by the variety of terms used in the Middle Ages to denote, apparently, the same thing. With regard to tournaments there are many such terms, mostly to be met with in their Latin or French forms: *torneamentum, justae, hastiludum* and *burdica* in Latin, or *tournois, joustes, behourds,* and *pas d'armes* in French. The first term we have discussed; the others need a bit of definition. A joust is a single combat between two warriors; it might be fought on horseback with lance, sword, axe, or dagger, or on foot with the same weapons. At first its spelling derived from its Latin form, *just.* The French softened the vowel, spelling it *jouste* and pronouncing it *joost.* The English used the same word, but as time went on and jousting was remembered only as an antiquated sport, the word went out of use—except as a sort of linguistic curiosity. It eventually came to be pronounced from disuse—or rather, mispronounced—as it is today. To match the sound of the word today, we might phonetically spell it as *jowst.*

The word *hastiludum* means spear-play or spear-game, and thus refers to the same thing as *joust,* in England sometimes called "spear-running." *Burdica* or *behourd* has so far eluded precise definition; in the early Middle Ages we find it used as an alternative for *joust*. Later, in the fourteenth century, it seems to refer to a sort of diminutive tournament. We are told that before it takes place there is no official "cry"– that is, the *burdica* seems to have been a sort of spontaneous affair, decided upon on the spur of the moment and not ceremonially advertised beforehand. The tournament at Runnymede would have been a *behourd* under that definition.

The *pas d'armes* was one of the favorite ways of "winning worship" in the age of chivalry. Knights-errant would sometimes camp out by a bridge or in a narrow pass and hold it against all-comers: whoever wanted to cross the bridge or get by first had to try his skill against the holder of the pass. This activity might sound like the action of a highwayman, but no one had to fight if they did not want to. Of course, the adversary had to be of knightly rank. The knight-errant sometimes participated in this enterprise either to discharge himself of a vow or to give himself a chance to get some ransom money. Occasionally he participated for the love of his lady. For the same reasons, most traveling knights would stop and climb into their armor and gratefully engage in the *pas*. Whoever won, both would gain honor and experience. That's how it was in the early days of the twelfth century. Later, from the middle of the thirteenth century, the making and holding of an artificial "pass" became one of the regular acts in a tournament, though the informal roadside effort of the knight-errant continued as long as chivalry lasted.

Another term, which came into use later than

the others and seems to have originated in England, needs some explication. It was probably inspired by the legends of King Arthur: "The knightly game called The Round Table." It seems the Round Table was held purely as a pastime, with only blunted weapons called "arms of courtesy" being used, and taking place in circular lists. These Round Table games were always followed by a feast provided for the guests by the magnate who "enterprised" the games.

As I said at the start of this chapter, in the early days tourneys were real fights, fought with real weapons. But sometime near the end of the twelfth century, we hear of lances being fitted with a special head shaped like a crown (called a "coronel" or "cronel"), while swords with rebated edges were used—that is, they were real swords without sharpened edges, and their points were rounded. These were the "arms of courtesy." By the middle of the thirteenth century, too, we find two sorts of jousts, called *à l'outrance* (to the death) or *à plaisance* (for fun). In the joust *à l'outrance* you fought with real weapons until someone was killed, disabled, or forced to surrender; in the

Fig. 27. Lance heads. A "cronel" for jousts à plaisance *and a sharp head for* à l'outrance

joust *à plaisance* your aim was to score more points, if you fought on foot, or to splinter your lance and unhorse your opponent if you fought on horse.

In the second half of the fourteenth century the tournament began to take on some of the elaboration that by the sixteenth century had made it little more than a pageant, fanciful and fantastic to the point of downright silliness. There is no space here to go into these elaborations in detail, but it's essential to offer a few examples.

In 1343 a tournament was held in London at Smithfield (a favorite place for tourneys in the thirteenth and fourteenth centuries, just as it became a favorite place for heretic-burnings in the sixteenth). In this tournament all the contestants entered the lists dressed as the pope and his cardinals. Later in 1393 the chronicler John de Trokelowe of St. Albans described the jousters at a tourney all turning up in the habits of monks. It was not until this time, the second half of the fourteenth century, that knights began to attend tournaments in fancy dress, though the idea of "The Unknown Knight," who arrived in disguise with a plain shield and his face hidden, is as old as the tournament concept itself and all its predecessors. At a tournament in 1383, again at Smithfield with Richard II in the royal box, there entered into the lists "threescore Ladyes of Honor mounted on fayre Palefreys rydynge on the oon side, richley appareled; and every Ladye led a Knyghte with a chayne of Silver, whyche knyghtes were apparelled to Joust." Eustache Deschamps, a poet of France, said in about

Fig. 28. "Every ladye led a Knyghte with a chayne of silver,
whyche knyghtes were apparelled to Joust."

1360: "Servants of love, look sweetly at these lovely
ones, angels of Paradise; then joust strong and joy-
ously and you will be honored and cherished." After
the tourney the ladies "took from their breasts divers
bunches of ribbons and garlands of silk to reward the
valor of these noble champions." But the winners
could rely on more solid prizes, often bags of gold or
rich jewels or fine horses—sometimes quite awkward
things. At the *behourd* at Runnymede that I've already
spoken of, the prize was a bear donated by the wife
of one of the barons present.

Great scandal sometimes resulted from these
tournaments. In the reign of Edward III of England

much public indignation was aroused by a band of females who went from tournament to tournament "in diverse and wonderful male apparel," according to the chronicler, who added that they were "ladies most costly and beautiful." In fact, evidence indicates that many great and noble ladies could joust as competently as their men. There are many references to such skillful ladies. Consider, for example, the incomparable Joan, Maid of France and Orleans, a splendid jouster who was exceptionally skilled with the lance. Many witnesses testified to her talents at her trial in 1432 and her rehabilitation twenty years later.

Early in the fifteenth century the tilt began being used in jousting. It was a long barrier extending the full length of the lists. At first the tilt was made of cloth hung from a cord, but later it consisted of light wood covered with cloth. The combatants rode one on each side, the idea being to afford extra protection and lessen the risk of the type of collision I described in Chapter I in the jousting between Jehan de Saintré and Sir Enquerrant de Cordona. Early in the fifteenth century, noblemen of sufficient wealth and standing began to have permanent tilts set up in the streets before their town houses. In Paris the Princes of the Blood and the chief officers of the Crown had their own tilts outside their palaces (hôtels, as they were called, to the great confusion of modern Englishmen). In castles and great houses built after about 1430 a tiltyard was an essential part of the building, and tiltyards were added to or adapted in old castles. In great cities like London, tournaments and jousts were often held in the streets. In London, Cheapside was a favorite place during the fourteenth and fifteenth centuries, and on more than one occasion a "solemn joust" was held on London Bridge.

In the year 1409 was born a regal connoisseur of romance—René, duc d'Anjou, king of Jerusalem and Sicily, count of Provence, poet, artist, and idealist as well as one of the leading nobles of France. His daughter Margaret of Anjou married Henry VI of England and became the mainspring of the Lancastrian cause during the Wars of the Roses. René wrote and illustrated with his own hand a splendid book called *A Treatise on the Form and Devising of a Tourney*, the most comprehensive authority on the tournament in the fifteenth century. He describes an imaginary tourney, similar to ones he organized and took part in many times.

What he describes provides firsthand, authoritative insight into the conducting of tournaments. At first the heralds of a great reigning noble arrive at the court of another reigning noble, presenting a challenge together with the names of the knights and judges taking part. The proposition is discussed, judges are appointed by the other side, and a date and place agreed upon. Then the tournament is proclaimed in many places (this is the "cry" I spoke of earlier), and all knights are invited. René then describes weapons and armor, horses and their caparisons. He describes the entry of the knights into the town where the tourney takes place. The towns-people are told to decorate their streets and windows. The knights, amid welcoming applause, ride into town grouped around their leaders, and all go to the house chosen for the feasting and dancing. Next day all the crested helms of the contestants are exhibited so that the judges and, of course, the ladies can see who has come to take part. In those days the names and records of most knights in Europe were known to many people. But it was part of the actual duty of the heralds, who were indispensable functionaries at even the smallest court, to know everything about everyone of "coat-armor." If it sounds like a tall order, it was; even so, the heralds were supposed to know. Thus, at the helm-viewing, heralds could denounce any knight presenting himself if his record were not clean, and they could disqualify him quiet-ly before the tournament began.

A *chevalier d'honneur* was then chosen. He was privileged to bear upon his lance the *couvre-chef de mercy*. The phrase "*couvre-chef*" literally means a head-scarf, similar to what is commonly worn today. The English called this scarf "kerchief," which later became "handkerchief." With this *couvre-chef de mercy*, the knight of honor could touch any knight in diffi-cult straits and so prevent further attacks on him. After the knight of honor was chosen, a day was assigned for the preliminary jousts. On the fourth day began the tourney proper—the mêlée. The her-alds cried, "lace your helms," and the knights rode into the lists under their leaders. Across the lists were stretched cords to keep the opposing teams apart. On a signal these cords were cut, and the combatants charged together, shouting their war cries and fighting until the president of the tournament threw down his warder (akin to a field-marshal's baton), which signaled the heralds to sound the retreat.

Then, after disarming and a good hot bath, feasting and dancing began. Do not believe the myth about medieval gentlefolk never washing; it's totally untrue. They were often steaming themselves in tubs of hot water when they could get it, or bathing in pools and rivers when they could not. What we seldom are led to believe, though it is true, is that the ladies would bathe the men, washing and drying them with skill and gentleness and attending to all their cuts and bruises. An essential part of a gentlewoman's training, besides housewifery, catering, needlework, weaving, cloth-making, dispensing medicines and all kinds of domestic science, was the basic training of a nurse.

The tournaments of the fifteenth century, by this time generally called *pas d'armes*, were often given fanciful names and rigged out with appropriate theatricals. Rene d' Anjou once held a *pas de la bergère*, where, in a curious foreshadowing of the court of Louis XV, all the ladies and gentlemen were dressed as shepherds and shepherdesses. The gallery was made to look like a thatched cottage, and the "queen of the tournament" was seen guarding her lambs. Two knights, the challengers, were shepherds. This event took place at Tarascon, on June 1, 1449, and is fully described in a song by Sir Loys de Beauveu, who took part. Similarly fanciful events were "The Emprise of the Dragon's Mouth," "of the Castle of Joyous Gard," and so on.

During this century the tournament more and more became just a game. For the settlement of serious points of honor or judicial processes, other forms were devised. The "combat of chivalry" was a duel fought either on horse or on foot with the weapons of war, carried on until one of the combatants could fight no more. It was a forerunner of the duels of the sixteenth and seventeenth centuries, and the successor of similar forms of single combat from remotest antiquity. The "combat of chivalry" was used for the settlement of affairs of honor, quite distinct from the "joust of peace," the judicial duel used to settle legal disputes. In fifteenth-century Germany they even settled legal quarrels between husband and wife in this way. It was, of course, simply a version of the ancient "trial by combat."

The final stage in the development of the tournament was reached in the Tudor period in English history. While all over Europe any sort of national festival or political happening was incomplete without a tournament, no keener supporter of these sports could be found than Henry VIII. When this Tudor king came to the throne in 1509 he was only nineteen, and no one could break a better lance. Throughout his reign he made sure jousting was one of the chief amusements of his court. He had permanent tilt-yards at Whitehall, Greenwich, and

Hampton Court. One of his chroniclers reports of an especially fine day of jousting for Henry: "The Kynge was that daie highlie to be praised, for he brake three and twenty spears besides atteints and bare down to grounde a man of arms and his horsse." Atteints were points scored by hitting the opponent without breaking the lance. An atteint on the head counted for more points than one on the body, and so on.

Even if games, tourneys were still dangerous. Charles Brandon, duke of Suffolk, wrote back to Henry VIII to describe the celebrations that took place when he carried Henry's sister Mary Tudor over to France to marry Louis XII. Suffolk tells of the jousting, noting that many were hurt therein "and one Frenchman is not like to live." A tournament in Paris in 1559 ended in high tragedy and put an end to serious jousting in France. The king, Henri II, was taking part, and after running the last course of the day he decided to run just one more course with a knight of Scotland, Gabriel de Montgomery. The Scot was reluctant to run against the king, but Henri persuaded him. They ran together, and Montgomery's lance hit the visor of the king's helmet, lifting it up as a splinter from the broken lance entered Henri's forehead over his right eye. He died of the wound ten days later.

Before this time, extra games had been added to tournaments, such as shooting (with a bow), wrestling, and "Casting the Barre," which was akin to Tossing the Caber. In fact, the tournament had become more like its modern successor, the military tournament. (I think Henry VIII would have approved of the naval field-gun competition.)

To get a sense of the range of activities at a tournament, consider a charming 1507 account of one of these events. A challenge was issued by those who called themselves the Servants of the Lady May, addressed to the Princess Margaret, daughter of Henry VII: "Most high and excellent Princess, under your patient supportacion I, which am called the Ladye Maie, of all moneths of the yeare to lusty hearts most pleasant..." The articles of the jousts that follow the challenge specify the contests: "The challenge of the Ladie Maie's servants, to all comers, to be performed at Greenwiche: to runne 8 cours: to shoot, standart-arrowe or Flight: to strike 8 strookes with Swords rebated: to wrestle all manner of wayes: to fight on foote with Spears rebated and afterwards to strike 8 strokes with Swords, with gripe or otherwise: to caste the Barre on Foote, and with the Arme, both heavie and light."

In England, tournaments were still held during the reign of King Charles I (1625-1649). But the English Civil War, pitting parliamentarians against the monarchy, put an end to official tournaments in the country. On the European continent, however, tournaments went on in a somewhat debased form until the eighteenth century. We hear of foot combats taking place at Dresden in 1719, for instance. But from the middle of the seventeenth century the old-style tournament was replaced by a sort of horse-show called the carousel, which was mainly a display of horsemanship, though it included such medieval survivals as running with lances at the ring or the quintain. While these survivals replaced the jousts, the old mêlée was replaced by the carousel proper, in which contestants, dressed in special light fancy dress armor, attempted with padded clubs and blunted swords to smash each other's crests. Though they fell short of the old tourneys of the thirteenth century, they helped form an almost unbroken link between medieval tournaments and the "Gothic" revival of the mid-nineteenth century. The most striking example of that link was the imitation tournament organized in the manner of the fifteenth century and held at Eglinton one rainy day in 1839. Some of the special armor made for this tournament still exists. It is, for its period, very credible imitation late fifteenth century armor of German style, made even by a German firm. Some of this armor and many of the lances made for the occasion still survive.

Tournament Armor

In the early days of chivalry, tournaments were fought in ordinary war-harness. But as tourney rules became more ceremonious—and because many valuable lives were lost needlessly—special armor and special weapons were adopted. The blunted lance-head (the cronel) first appeared in about 1180-90, and at the same time it became respectable in some circles to use unsharpened swords. Nearly a century later we find that swords even more harmless, made of whalebone, were used in tourneys, for even an unsharpened medieval sword was a pretty deadly weapon. Keep in mind: a sharpened sword has an edge like a razor and, as we've seen, can do severe damage. The earliest mention of whalebone swords is in the royal accounts for furnishing a tournament at Windsor in 1278; helms and armor made of leather were listed as well. Seventeen years later a commission of the great barons of England drew up "Statutes of Arms" to regulate the armor and weapons used in tournaments:

. . . No son of a great lord, that is to say of an Earl or Baron, shall have other armor than mufflers and cuishes, and spaudlers, and a skull-cap; without more; and shall not wear a Dagger or Sword pointed, nor mace, but only a broadsword. And if any be found who, in either of these points, shall offend against the Statute, he shall lose his horse whereon he is mounted that day, and be imprisoned for one year.

And they who shall come to see the Tournament shall not be armed with any manner of armor, and shall bear no sword, or dagger, or staff, or mace, or stone, upon such forfeiture as in the case of Esquires aforesaid; and no Groom or Footman shall bear Sword, or Dagger, or Staff, or Stone, and if they be found offending they shall be imprisoned for seven years.

These were wise and sensible precautions made in a real effort to prevent loss of life, foreshadowing the more sporting tourneys of the fourteenth and fifteenth centuries. Some of the armor mentioned in these statutes is a little hard to identify; some very odd theories have been put forward to define the word "mufflers," for instance. It was suggested that this referred to special armor made of wool, presumably like layers of knitted sweaters. Mufflers, of course, is the name given in the thirteenth century to mail gloves made like mitts as an extension of the sleeve of the hauberk. The requirement that these be used in tournaments is because, by 1295, plated gauntlets had already come into use.

Fig. 29. Armor of about 1450, showing the lance rest fastened to the right side of the breastplate. You can see the big circular plate (vamplate) on the lance, to protect the hand. These did not come into use until about 1380 to 1400

In an English manuscript dating from about 1330 we see knights jousting with what appear to be small padded bolsters fastened to their saddle-bows and projecting downward to protect their legs, like the shin-guards on a motor-bike (The Treatise of Walter de Milemete, Nobilitatibus, Sapientiis et Prudentiis Regum. Christ Church library, Oxford.) Fifty years later similar guards made either of wood or of metal plates were made as part of a special type of saddle for jousting.

Not until about 1425 is a clear distinction made between ordinary field armor (or Hosting Harness) and tilting armors. (After the introduction of the tilt in the 1420s, the word tilting was commonly used for jousting.) As the fifteenth century wore on, highly specialized tournament armor developed. The earliest definite mentioning of this specialized armor is in a manuscript by an anonymous French writer, dated 1446. It describes in detail the body armor worn for jousting, item by item:

(1) A cuirass or brigandine with a lance-rest (fig. 29) and special buckles to which the helm and other pieces could be fastened.

(2) For the left hand a main de fer (iron hand), called by the English manifer, a gauntlet "made of one piece, and guards the hand and the arm up to 3 fingers above the elbow."

(3) A pauldron of one piece for the left shoulder.

(4) For the right hand a small gauntlet called a gagnepain, meaning breadwinner, a name once applied in the twelfth century to a knight's sword.

(5) Above the gagnepain, an arm-defense called, from its shape, *epaule de mouton* (shoulder of mutton), which in England was called a poldermitten. It was a complete hinged covering for the forearm with a large plate like a shell covering the outside of the elbow, curving in over the bend of it and out over the lower part of the upper arm (fig. 35).

(6) On the right shoulder a small laminated pauldron with a large besagew in front. A besagew was a flat disc of metal hung from the shoulder to

cover the gap under the arm (fig. 35).

(7) A contraption made of padded leather like the fend-off on a yacht, called poire (pear) because of its shape. It hung from the left shoulder and served as a shock absorber between the breast and the shield.

(8) The shield itself, a small, rectangular, concave defense made of stout wood covered with leather or plates of horn.

The writer goes on to say that, in France, leg harness was generally worn with this armor, which suggests that the French didn't use the high saddle with leg-guards that was popular in Germany, England, and the Low Countries at this time.

Most of our knowledge of jousting (which is very scanty) is from German sources, so we are better informed about the manner of its development there. Its earliest specialized form, breaking away from the old international and universal style of jousting, appears about 1380-90 and was called Hohenzeuggestech. In Germany the word gestech was always used to refer to jousting with blunt lances, and this word means literally high armor joust. The most distinctive characteristic of this type of joust was the use of a special saddle, one much higher than the ordinary war saddle and rising in a narrow

Fig. 30. Saddle for the Hohenzeuggestech, c. 1440. Tower of London Armouries

91

Fig. 31. Knight apparelled for the Deutsches Gestech course, about 1510.
He wears a special jousting armor like the one shown in figure 35, and
his horse's chest and his own legs are protected by great padded Stechsack
which you can see under the horse's bard

ridge about ten inches above the horse's back. In
front, protecting the rider from his feet to his waist,
were leg-guards in the form of a forked shield over
the horse's withers (fig. 30). Back from this shield-like
saddle-bow extended on either side a flat, curved
wooden bar that held the rider's thighs and prevented him from being thrown from his saddle.

Ordinary field-armor would have been worn with this saddle. Instead of a visored helmet used in war, a more open helm would have been worn. This kind of gestech seems to have fallen out of favor by about 1450 and was succeeded by a kind called *deutsches gestech* to distinguish it from the Italian style fought with a tilt, which the Germans didn't use. Instead, they protected their horses from collision with an enormous padded stechsack like a great bolster around the horse's chest and shoulders. This served to protect the rider's legs too (fig. 31).

We are perhaps more familiar with the jousting helm than with any other piece of armor, for it (or something meant to represent it) appears as a crest on most coats of arms. Helms *pro torniamentis* are mentioned as early as 1268, but we are uncertain

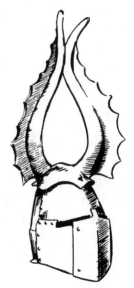

Fig. 32. Helm in the Kunsthistorisches Museum in Vienna. This once belonged to the Austrian family of von Pranck and was made in about 1380. You can see the reinforcing plate on the left hand side of the visor, bending round a little way over the right side. The great crest of leather is the original one, and is very rare

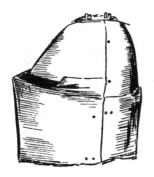

Fig. 33. Helm (once belonging to Sir Nicholas Hanberk?) in Cobham Church, Kent. About 1400-1410. This is very similar to the helm of Henry V in Westminster Abbey

what form tournament helms took then. We are certain of the helms for tourneys used about a century later. There are two helms of about 1380, one in Vienna and one in Copenhagen, which have heavy reinforcing pieces on the left side (figure 32). The helm of Henry V in Westminster Abbey has similar reinforcement, so perhaps these should be regarded as jousting helms, not war-helms. From helms like Henry V's developed the so-called "frog-mouthed" tilting helm that we know so well. Figure 33 will give you some idea of what this type of helm looked like. A later and larger variety of helm, called a *stechhelm*, is shown in Figure 34. These great helms had elaborate padded linings laced into them with arming-points.

During the last quarter of the fifteenth century the two best-known styles of tilting armor developed. Several examples of both kinds survive: armors for the *gestech*, a German and an Italian fashion, and armors for the *scharfrennen*, a course run with sharpened lances. Figure 35 shows a splendid example of a German armor of the first kind, made in about 1480, which you can see in the Wallace Collection in London. This armor was heavy, but that apparently didn't matter since a knight only had to wear it for

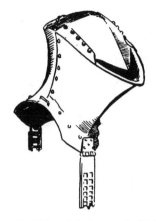 

Fig. 34. Helm, of the German Stechhelm type but of English make. About 1475. Tower of London Armouries. Notice the metal straps (called Charnels) with which the helm was fastened to staples on the breast and backplates

Fig. 35. Complete armor for the joust (Deutsches Gestech), German, about 1485. Wallace Collection, London

short periods and hardly needed to move at all. The Italian style for this kind of armor was similar but ugly. The helms have none of the graceful curves shown by the German *stechhelm*, but look like enormous pill-boxes (figure 36).

Lighter armor of a totally different kind was used for the *scharfrennen*. The head was protected by a sallet and bevor, similar to but stouter than those used in war. On the body was only a light half-armor or a brigandine, and arms and legs were unarmored. A large wood-and-leather shield covered the left side and left arm, while the great vamplate of the lance protected the right arm (figure 37). These vamplates, incidentally, were never used before the middle of the fourteenth century and only rarely before the

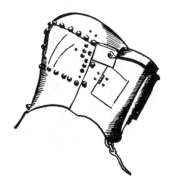

Fig. 36. Jousting helm of Italian style. Once belonged to Gasparo Fracasso, Milanese Ambassador to the Imperial Court at Vienna. About 1490. Kunsthistorisches Museum, Vienna

middle of the fifteenth. Even so, we constantly find less-careful modern illustrators and film technical advisers giving their twelfth- and thirteenth-century knights these vamplates, quite anachronistically.

Leg harness was not worn in the *scharfrennen.* Instead, long laminated tassets (fig. 37), foreshadowing those so commonly used in the early seventeenth century, protected the knight's thighs; large plates, called tilting sockets (fig. 38), were hung from the waist as an extra defense on either side. A heavier than usual lance was used for the *scharfrennen*; it couldn't be inclined over the horse's neck as in the ordinary joust, so the contestants had to run together right side to right side. The shaft was too thick to hold, so the jouster held it in the great queue (shown in figures 35 and 37) and directed his lance with a small handle inside the vamplate.

These *gestech* and *scharfrennen* armors continued in use until about 1540-50. After the middle of the sixteenth century a new fashion arose, particularly in the productions of the Royal Armories at Greenwich. Extra pieces for the joust, called in England "pieces of advantage" or "double pieces," were added to ordinary field-armors. At first merely reinforcing pieces for the left side, these attachments rapidly developed into so many extras that, from a basic armor, half a dozen armors for different sorts of combat could be devised. Such a collection was called a garniture, or a suit of armor. That is what a suit of armor actually is, not the popularly supposed simple complete armor, which, until about 1620, was simply called an armor or a harness.

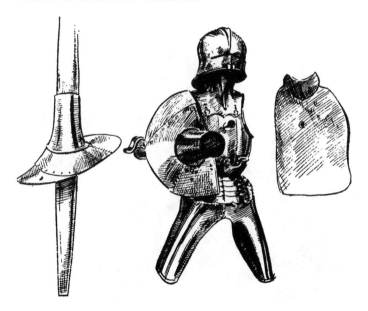

Fig. 37. Armor for the scharfrennen. The wood and leather shield (shown to the right) is fastened by the bolt in the center of the breastplate. The vamplate of the extra-large size lance is semi-circular and far larger than the ordinary gestech vamplate, and is swept backwards (see the side-view of it to the left) to protect the chest and shoulder. In this course, which was run right side to right side, the horses were blindfolded (with eyeless metal chanfrons, or fabric bards) so that they would not swerve

97

Fig. 38. Knight apparelled for the scharfrennen. You can see the "tilting sockets" covering his legs, the blindfold bard, and the long "queue" to take the end of the lance. There is no armor on his right arm, for the vamplate will protect it

There were some special armors for jousts fought on foot, but, since they have nothing to do with horses, I won't discuss them here.

Of course, in a period as fascinating, popular, and distant as the Middle Ages, inaccurate beliefs surely will creep up and be annoyingly persistent in the modern mindset. I would like to mention six common misconceptions about medieval life and war that you should be clear about.

(1) There is no such thing as chain-mail. It is mail, and has been called mail in England since the Norman Conquest. Chain-mail is a silly, unnecessary double-word invented by nineteenth-century writers, and has no place in the true study of armor.

(2) Armor was not excessively heavy. It was meant to be worn comfortably. The weapons used with it were not very heavy either. A listing of weights of armor begins on page 103.

(3) Knights did not have to be hoisted into their saddles with cranes. Perhaps if they were old, wounded, or tired they had to be helped up or they used a mounting-block, but never, never did they use cranes. This notion is inane and, even if once funny, is funny no more.

(4) A knight's war-horse was not like a cart-horse, nor did it trot. Have you ever noticed how circus-horses move when someone rides bareback standing up? If the horses don't go at a slow canter, they run, just like a medieval war-horse.

(5) Lances did not have a metal vamplate pro-

tecting the hand until after about 1400. They did not have a specially narrowed grip until 1450. They were just long straight shafts tapering a little toward the point.

(6) You did not need a spanner and screwdriver to get into your armor, nor a tin-opener to get out. It was very carefully and simply designed and fitted, fastening with straps and buckles, or, after 1500, sometimes with little spring catches.

Unfortunately you will encounter those mistaken notions in many places, in history books and historical novels, in dramatic works (but not if Shakespeare wrote the play) and in films, and surely on the television screen. But they are wrong; they are a disservice not only to the medieval knight and his legacy, but to the truth.

Appendix I

Monetary Values

It is almost impossible to compare the buying power of medieval money with modern values. What we can say, admittedly vaguely, is that some things bought in 1300 for the equivalent of one dollar, for instance, could likely cost $500 or more today (keep in mind that the dollar was not the currency of exchange in medieval Europe). Inflation is a discriminatory creature, being harsher on some products and services than on others. Medical costs in America, for instance, have risen astronomically in just the last thirty years, while the costs of other services have risen less dramatically. Beware, then, that to make a generalization about how monetary values have changed from medieval times to the present is a precarious enterprise at best.

The commonest medieval money unit seems to have been the mark. Used all over Europe, the mark denoted a standard weight of gold or silver. In England after 1066 the mark was stabilized at 160 silver pennies. The pound (symbol £) was the chief money unit in England from Saxon times onward

101

(and is still used today). By the time of Elizabeth I, it had fallen to one-third of its original value; and its purchasing power has been declining ever since (you could buy more with a pound in medieval England than you can today). Despite the decline in purchasing power, the value of the pound was given a fixed standard in 1601 that remained in use until 1931.

In France the livre was the chief monetary unit. Around A.D. 800 the value of the livre was fixed at 400 grams of silver. By the fourteenth century, the livre had fallen to one-eighth of this value and, 200 years later, to one-twentieth.

A cold accounting of coinage, currency, and monetary units doesn't really help us to appreciate the value of things like horses and armor in medieval times. It may be fairly safe to say that a good complete armor in 1460 would have about the same value as a good small car today; and, as you can see from this book, the values of horses have not changed a great deal.

Appendix II

The Weight of Armor

Well-made fifteenth-century fighting armor (called "field armor" or "hosting harness") weighed no more than the uniform and equipment of many army units up to about 1910. Indeed, as late as the 1960s, the full ceremonial uniform and equipment of some English troopers weighed a little more than a full armor of 1460. Most of the weight of the full apparel of the twentieth-century fighting man emanated from the shoulders, whereas the weight in medieval armor was fairly evenly distributed over all parts of the body.

Of course, jousting armor and seventeenth-century "musketproof" armor were much heavier than field armor. The table on the next two pages shows some comparative weights selected at random.

COMPLETE ARMORS

Italian field armor, c. 1450 (Scott Collection, Glasgow), 57 pounds.
German field armor, c. 1525 (Wallace Collection, London, 41 pounds 13½ ounces.
German field armor, Pancraz von Freyburg (Wallace Collection, London), 56 pounds 4½ ounces.
Field armor, Greenwich, 1590 (Wallace Collection, London), 71 pounds 14 ounces.
"Cuirassier" (musket-proof) armor, c. 1620-30 (Schloss Churburg, Tyrol), 69 pounds 5 ounces.
"Gestech" (jousting) armor, German, c. 1500 (Wallace Collection, London), 90 pounds 1½ ounces.

HELMETS

Helm, English, The Black Prince, c 1370 (Canterbury Cathedral), 7 pounds, 2 ounces.
Bascinet (visored) and camail, c. 1390 (Schloss Churburg, Tyrol), 12 pounds 9 ounces.
Armet, Italian, c. 1470 (Wallace Collection, London), 7 pounds 7 ounces.
Sallet, German, c. 1470 (Wallace Collection, London), 5 pounds.
Jousting helm, English, c. 1480 (Tower of London Armories), 23 pounds 8 ounces.

MAIL

Long hauberk, 14th century (Royal Scottish Museum, Edinburgh), 31 pounds.

Short hauberk, 14th century (Schloss Churburg, Tyrol), 20 pounds 11 ounces.

HORSE ARMOR

German, Pancraz von Freyburg (Wallace Collection, London), 66 pounds 5½ ounces.

Probably English-made, Henry VIII, 1514-19 (Tower of London Armories), 69 pounds 3 ounces.

Bibliography

Blair, Claude. *European Armour.* London, 1958.

Camp, S J. and Mann, Sir James. *European Arms and Armour.* 3 vols. Wallace Collection Catalogues. London, 1920-1945.

Clephan, R. C. *The Tournament: Its Periods and Phases.* London, 1919.

Cripps Day, F. H. *A History of the Tournament in England and France.* London, 1918.

ffoulkes, C. J. *The Armourer and his Craft from the 11th to the 15th Century.* London, 1912.

Gay, Victor. *Glossaire Archetologique du Moyen Age et du Renaissance.* Paris, 1882-1928.

Harmand, Adrien, *Jeanne d'Arc: Ses Costumes,* Son Armure. Paris, 1929.

Laking, Sir G. F. *A Record of European Armor and Arms through Seven Ages.* 5 vols. London, 1920-1922.

Mann, Sir James. *European Arms and Armour,* 2 vols. Wallace Collection Catalogues. London, 1962.

Megnin, Pierre. *Histoire du Harnachement et de la Ferrure du Cheval.* Vincennes, 1904.

PERIODICALS

The following deal with arms and armor, and occasionally contain material concerning horses, tournaments, tournament armor, and horse armor:

American Arms Collector. Towson, Md, 1957 (in progress).
Armf Antichi. Bolletino del 'Arcademia di S. Marciano. Turin, 1954 (in progress).
Joumal of the Arms and Armour Society. London, 1953 (in progress).
Livrustkammaren. Journal of the Royal Armoury of Stockholm. 1937 (in progress).
Svenska Vapenhistoriske Aarskrft. Journal of the Swedish Arms and Armour Society. Stockholm (in progress).
Vaabenhistoriske Aarbøger. Journal of the Danish Arms and Armour Society. Copenhagen (in progress).
Zeitschrift fur Historische Waffen- und Kostumkunde. Quarterly organ of the-now defunct Verein fur Historische Waffenktmde. 17 vols. Dresden and Berlin, 1897-1944. Now revived as the quarterly organ of the Gesellschaft fur Historische Waffen- und Kostiimkunde. 1959 (in progress).

Glossary

Adrianople - Site in Thrace (see below) near where Goths defeated the legions of Rome in a great battle in 376. Using fierce charges by a mass of horsemen, the Goths were able to trounce the highly trained legionaries. After this battle, the Romans took many Gothic cavalrymen into their pay as mercenaries. A Goth-inspired method of fighting thus began to prevail in most of Europe.

Alfred the Great - king of the West Saxons from 871 to 899. His leadership helped keep Wessex, the land of the West Saxons, from being overcome by Danish invaders.

Anglo-Saxon Conquest - invasion of Britain by Germanic tribes in the early part of the fifth century A.D. This conquest involved three groups of invaders, the Jutes, the Angles, and the Saxons, and was in many ways an extension of a mass migration of Germanic peoples that had begun hundreds of years before - the movement from northeast Europe into areas of the Roman Empire. The Jutes, from Jutland, settled in Kent.

Anhalt - former state in central Germany. The great German family of Anhalt held, until 1926, a bard for horses that was used in battle and was made about 1480, probably for Waldemar VI, duke of Anhalt-Zerbst, who reigned from 1473 to 1508.

Arçon - front of war-saddle that curves upward. It is the wooden framework of the medieval saddle, also called the saddle tree.

Arquebus - a portable firearm, also referred to as a harquebus. It is obsolete.

Arquebusier - one who wields a portable firearm.

Atteints - during a medieval joust, atteints were points scored by hitting the opponent without breaking the lance. How many points were awarded depended on where the hit occurred, with the head worth more points than the body.

Barded horses - horses covered with fabric or armor.

Battle of Hastings - fought between Saxon and Norman soldiers in 1066 in a valley north of Hastings in Sussex. It occurred on the field of Senlac. The Saxon side was led by Harold, earl of Sussex; the Norman side was led by William, duke of Normandy. At stake was the kingship of England, which became an issue when Edward the Confessor died childless in January of that year. William's side triumphed in what has been known to history as the Norman Conquest (see below).

Bayeux Tapestry - stitched by women needleworkers, it provides a story in picture form of details leading up to and including the Norman Conquest (see below). An idea of the first medieval saddles can be glimpsed from the tapestry.

Behourd - in the early Middle Ages, it was another word for *joust.* It later seems to have been used to refer to smaller, less formal tournaments in which no official "cry" was sounded at the beginning. It was a spontaneous affair. Also called burdica.

Belisarius - great Byzantine general who lived from circa A.D. 505 to 565.

Bevor - face-guarding, head-protecting piece of armor worn with a helmet. Also spelled "beaver."

Bit - mouthpiece of a bridle (see below). The lower ends of the cheek bands, which pass along the horse's cheeks, are attached to the bit. The bit enables the rider to signal his or her intentions to the horse.

Black Prince - Edward Plantagenet, Prince of Wales, an impressive, skilled commander whose fiery genius helped the English defeat the French at Poitiers in 1356. He was the eldest son of Edward III .

Breast-strap - a broad band across the horse's chest that prevents the saddle from slipping backward.

Bridle - headgear for a horse consisting of the bit and the reins.

Bridoon - British word for snaffle bit; bridoon often indicates a snaffle bit with a larger than normal mouthpiece.

Brigandine - body armor made of plates or scales and having a fabric or leather covering.

Briton - one of the groups of people in Britain prior to the Anglo-Saxon Conquest (see above) that began in the fifth century A.D.

Burdica - see behourd (above).

Burr-plate - a wide front plate on a saddle that protected the rider from the waist almost to the knees.

Byzantine Empire - Eastern Roman Empire that emerged after the Western Empire collapsed in A.D. 476.

Caballero - Spanish word for a gentleman, horseman, knight.

Cantle - back portion of a saddle. During the thirteenth century it spread forward to embrace the rider's hips.

Caparison - another name for bard (see barded horses above), though *caparison* more specifically refers to rich, colorful trappings covering a horse.

Caracole - a battle tactic that developed during the sixteenth century. To employ the tactic, a troop on horse would move to within pistol shot of its opponent. The front rank would fire, then peel off to the left and to the right to allow the second rank to fire, which would do the same to allow the third rank to fire, and so on.

Carousel - a type of horse show that, from the middle of the seventeenth century, replaced the old-style tournament. Though it mainly involved a display of horsemanship, it included running with lances at the ring or quintain.

Cataphractoi - Roman soldiers in armor.

Cavalière - Italian word for knight or horseman.

Chanfron - plate armor to protect a horse's head.

Chanson - in general, French poems to be sung, though in the twelfth and thirteenth centuries they referred to love poems.

Chansons de geste - beginning forms of French epic poetry, they told of heroic deeds.

Charles VI of France - lived from 1368 until 1422, this son of Charles V ruled well until suffering from bouts with insanity circa 1392. He became king in 1380 while in his minority, during part of which the country's affairs were run by a regent, his uncle, Louis, duke of Anjou. Charles VI assumed active control in 1388. The devastating French defeat at Agincourt, against England and its king, Henry V, occurred in 1415. An entry in an inventory of Charles VI in 1411 includes armor for man and horse.

Chausses - tight-fitting armor for the legs and feet usually made of mail.

Cheapside - a favorite town in London to hold tournaments.

Cheek bands - two long straps that pass along the horse's cheeks and are fastened to the bit.

Chevalier - French word for knight.

Chevalier d'honneur - as described in *A Treatise on the Form and Devising of a Tourney,* during the fifteenth century a knight of honor would be chosen for a tournament; he would bear a scarf or kerchief on his lance with which he could bring mercy to a struggling knight during the tournament. If a knight were hopelessly losing, the *chevalier d'honneur* had the power to touch him with the scarf and thus signal that no further attacks should be unleashed upon the struggling knight. See below, *couvre-chef de mercy* and Rene, duc d'Anjou.

Chivalry - in its broadest sense, it refers to the class of medieval knights, but the meaning of the word *chivalry* evolved to signify the qualities the ideal knight should embrace: chiefly honor and courtesy. In this sense, chivalry refers to the code of conduct governing the behavior of knights.

Cinque Ports - group of English maritime towns in Sussex and Kent. They would help in the country's sea defense in exchange for certain benefits.

Cniht - the old Anglo-Saxon word meaning a young man of good family. It is the word from which derived the modern word *knight.* Unlike the word for knight in Italian, Spanish, French, and German, the English word does not derive from a word for horse, perhaps because, unlike in other countries, in England before the Norman Conquest of 1066 (see below), the warrior classes did not fight on horseback.

Coif - covering for the head and neck.

Colonna, Fabrizio - died in early sixteenth century, he was grand constable of Naples and a leading general. He was one of numerous important members of the Colonna family, a noble Roman family that began its ascent toward social, political, and religious power in the early twelfth century.

Coronel - a special head shaped like a crown that some lances were fitted with. Also called "cronel." These lances, along with swords that did not have sharpened edges, were "arms of courtesy." They were used to joust *à plaisance.*

Courser - a swift horse trained for the hard, long work of war.

Couvre-chef de mercy - a headscarf or kerchief placed upon the lance of a knight of honor at a fifteenth-century tournament. If another knight were struggling, the knight of honor could bring mercy by touching the struggling knight with the *couvre-chef de mercy,* thus preventing further attacks upon him. See *chevalier d'honneur.*

Crinet - armor that guarded a horse's neck.

Cronel - see "coronel."

Crupper - loop that goes under a horse's tail and is fastened to the saddle to prevent it from sliding forward.

"Cry" - proclamation made in many places to announce that a tournament is to take place.

Cuirass - plate armor protecting the breast and back.

Curb - a bit mouthpiece; also refers to inflammation that may occur in the back of a horse's legs.

Dagged - notched edges giving a decorative look to medieval garb.

Dauphin - oldest son of a French king.

De Nesle, Raoul - constable of France who fell in the battle of Courtrai in 1302, in which Flemish burghers trounced French knights who had occupied Flanders. An inventory of armor and weapons left by de Nesle refers to the use of defensive pieces for the flanks and crupper (see above).

De Previlly, Geoffrey - a baron of Anjou who is credited with inventing the *Conflictus Gallicus* or, as it is also known, the *Bataille Francais.*

Destrier - the ultimate knightly horse, tall and majestic, trained to perform in jousts with courage and skill.

Edward I - king of England who lived from 1239 to 1307. Considered a courageous, strong leader, a great warrior king who saw the tremendous combat possibilities of the Welsh longbow.

Edward III - ascended to the throne of England in 1327 at the age of 15. He was the grandson of Edward I and the son of the ineffectual Edward II, who was no warrior, suffered great losses at the hands of the Scots, and was murdered by his barons. Edward III had a great desire to unite Scotland and England. He realized that, since the French often aided the Scots, he would have to fight the French first. Edward III's kingship thus ushered in the Hundred Years' War (1337-1453).

Exchequer - British agency overseeing public monies. Henry I officially established the Exchequer as a governmental department in the twelfth century, though the Treasury had been around before then.

Fete - type of village fair or festival.

Fetlocks - armor which protects the back of a horse's leg just over the hoof.

Flanchard - part of a horse's armor protecting the center of one side of the horse.

Gagnepain - a small gauntlet worn in jousts to protect the hand.

Garnisseur - French word for trimmer of clothes; some statues drawn up in 1403 to regulate the work of saddlers indicate that *garnisseurs* covered the inside of saddles with sheepskin and the outside with velvet or leather.

Gauntlet - a heavy glove worn to protect the hand in combat.

Gineta - Spanish word for jennet, a smaller horse greatly favored by ladies during the Middle Ages. Despite its size, this type of horse was used for fighting in medieval Spain.

Ginetour - name for horsemen in Spain in the fifteenth and early sixteenth centuries.

Goths - Teutons (see Teutonic below) who raided parts of the Roman Empire in the third through fifth centuries. Goths won a significant victory over Roman soldiers in 376 (see Adrianople above). The Gothic fighting method involved intense, powerful charges of horsemen. It would come to shape and define European war methods.

Hackney - in modern times the Hackney refers to a type of harness horse, a trotter. But from the medieval times onward, a hackney (lowercase) became a general term for a riding horse.

Hastiludum - word for "spear play," the running together of two lance-wielding foes on horseback; it is another word for *joust.*

Hauberk - tunic or coat, it was long and often reached the knees; made of leather or of mail, it served as defensive protection for a warrior.

Headpiece - as its name implies, a covering for the head; it was part of a horse's armor.

Headstall - part of the bridle going around the horse's head.

Henry the Fowler - first of the Saxon line of kings of Germany, he ruled from 919 until his death in 936. A strong leader, he was considered, though never officially crowned, one of the emperors of the Holy Roman Empire. Some evidence suggests tournaments involving knights and horses were held in Germany as early as 842. Henry, who lived from 876 to 936, organized many during his lifetime.

Heraldic device - family crest or coat of arms on a shield or above the helmet.

Heralds - representatives of kings and lords. One of their duties was to announce the names of the tournaments' contestants.

Hôtel - a tiltyard outside of a palace.

Jennet - smallish horse that was favored by ladies during the Middle Ages. It seems to have been Spanish in origin. See *gineta* (above).

Joan of Arc - known as the Maid of Orléans, she lived from 1412 to 1431. She was an extremely talented jouster whose skill with the lance was exceptional. France's national heroine, her life was far from calm, even though she believed either angels' voices or God directed her at first to lead a pious life. Those voices eventually led her to guide France during turbulent times.

Joust - a combat with lances between two knights on horseback, the joust was the noblest and most admired exercise among all the knightly arts of combat. Though different types of jousting developed, its essential requirement remained: it involved the running together of two horse-riding combatants with long lances. It called for exceptional military and equestrian skill. Horses had to be trained to ride in jousts, for the animal's skill and courage were important to the success of the knight in a joust.

Joust à l'outrance - to joust *à l'outrance* was to joust to the death.

Joust à plaisance - to joust *à plaisance* was to joust for pleasure

King Arthur - figure around whom many medieval romances were written, thus giving him a legendary stature. He is said to have created the Knights of the Round Table. The legendary figure is probably based on a real sixth-century king of the Britons.

Knight - a medieval warrior whose social standing was often reflected by the type of horse or horses he rode. The ideal medieval knight was generally of noble birth and a tough fighter but also a polite, useful, and capable member of society.

Knight banneret - a knight distinguished and respected enough to be able to bring a group of followers into a fight under his own banner.

Knight-errant - a wandering knight who did not swear permanent allegiance to a lord; instead, the knight-errant traveled, seeking adventure where he could find it. Though some knights-errant were romantic souls trying to right wrongs, many in the twelfth and thirteenth centuries were tough professional fighters who needed to compete in tournaments as a way of making a living.

Legionary - member of a legion, soldier of a legion.

List - an arena for jousting.

Livre - former French monetary unit issued as coins, first in gold, then in silver, and finally in copper. It ceased being used in the late eighteenth century.

Mace - weapon that started in remote times as a club and eventually developed into an armor-piercing device. It was of many shapes, some beautiful in style.

Mail - armor that was flexible, consisting of rings linked together or of small exterior plates.

Manifer - a gauntlet made of one piece for the left hand which guarded the hand and arm just above the elbow.

Marshal - highest military officer in France.

Martingale - piece of equestrian equipment for steadying a horse's head. It often involves a strap attached to the girth, going through the forelegs, and ending in two rings. The reins are fed through these rings.

Minster - city on the island of Sheppey, in the county of Kent, in England.

Norman Conquest - the overtaking of Anglo-Saxon England by Norman leader William the Conqueror in 1066. It had great significance, socially and linguistically. William gave British land belonging to Saxon nobles to Norman barons and earls. The Normans spoke French and made that language the daily language of the government. While many high-ranking people and clergy spoke French and Latin, hordes of common people continued speaking English, and so the language survived (but not without evolving). Considering the prominence of English today - and the disuse of Latin - Geoffrey Chaucer's decision to write in English has proven to be a most prescient and wise move.

Ornamental boss - a decorative stud or knob on a horse's bit.

Palfrey - a noble horse by birth and training, the preferred mount for hunting and traveling. The palfrey had a gentler disposition than the destrier (see above).

Pauldron - plate armor used to protect the shoulder.

Peytral - decorative piece of horse armor for defense of the animal's breast. Also called *poitrel.*

Pistol - after about 1535 a small handgun was perfected that, in the 1540s, became known as a pistol. It is a short firearm.

Pistoleers - armored horsemen carrying three pistols each. After riding at an adversary, troops of pistoleers would fire their pistols and then rush in with their swords. Developed in the sixteenth century, this fighting tactic was fine in theory but ineffective and even disastrous in practice.

Poldermitten - part of the body armor worn for jousting, it functioned as an arm defense. It completely covered the forearm, elbow and upper arm. The word poldermitten is a linguistic corruption of the French word *epaule de mouton* (shoulder of mutton).

Procopius - wrote a history of the mid-sixth-century Gothic wars. Procopius was secretary of the great Byzantine general Belisarius (see above).

Queue - a tail fitted to the backplate of armor, it projected about a foot or more out of the right side of the back.

Reins - strap of leather or rope attached to the bit in a horse's mouth which is used to contol the horse.

Ritter - German word for knight. Related to German word *Ritt*, which means "ride," thus showing the close tie between horsemanship and knighthood.

Roman Empire - one-time dominant world power; as an empire it was established in 27 B.C. and lasted in the West until roughly the fifth century A.D.

Round Table - Knightly game held purely as a pastime, with only blunted weapons called "arms of courtesy" being used, and taking place in circular lists. These games were always followed by a feast provided for the guests by the magnate who "enterprised" the games.

Rounsey - a strong horse, it was used in the cavalry for non-knightly men-at-arms or as a riding horse.

Saddletree - frame of a saddle; a wood or plastic base on which the saddle is constructed.

Sallet - light helmet, often with a faceguard. Along with the bevor, it protected the head and was worn especially during the *scharfrennen*, a type of joust conducted with sharpened lances.

Sarmatians - a race of people who moved westward into the grasslands of South Russia around the first century A.D. They were superb horsemen who rode heavy animals and who fought with the lance and the long sword, giving them an advantage over their nemesis, the Scythians (see below).

Scythians - the people of Scythia, ancient name of an area in southeast Europe and Asia. The Scythians rode small, quick-moving horses and shot bows from the saddle. They were defeated by the Sarmatians (see above).

Senlac - field where the Battle of Hastings was fought.

Serf - in feudal world, someone in servitude to a lord.

Sheppey - island in southeast England, part of the county of Kent.

Snaffle - a commonly used bit (see above) with a joint in the middle.

Stirrup - deliberately bent piece of metal, leather, or wood into which the rider's foot is placed - and which supports the foot - while riding a horse saddleback.

Tack - general term for the equipment used in riding horses, such as bridles, saddles, etc.

Tassets - armor protecting a knight's thighs.

Teutonic - pertaining to Teutons, ancient Germanic or Celtic people.

Thrace - in Southeast Europe in the Balkan peninsula, north of the Aegean Sea. In ancient times, it extended to the Danube.

Throat lash - thin strip of the bridle (see above) that passes beneath the horse's throat and helps keep the bridle in place.

Tilting sockets - large plates that were hung from the waist as an extra defense on either side of a knight's armor.

Trooper - horse-cavalry soldier; a policeman on horseback.

Trouvere - wandering singers or storytellers.

Vamplate - guard on the handle of some lances.

Varlet - a knight's attendant or page; a person of low rank within stratified society.

Warder - like a field-marshal's baton, which signaled the heralds to sound the retreat.

Wars of the Roses - fierce conflicts in England from 1455 to 1485 between the House of Lancaster and the House of York for control of the monarchy.

Wheel-lock - type of gun which consisted of a toothed wheel resembling a gear connected to a spring which was wound by a key. The trigger released the wheel which rubbed against a flint which showered sparks to ignite the gunpowder in the barrel.

Withers - back part of a horse located bwtween the shoulder blades.

Xenophon - Greek historian who was born in 431 B.C. and died circa 350 B.C. He fought with Athenian cavalry and was an experienced horseman. Among his works is the book *On Horsemanship*.

INDEX

Also in the Medieval Knight series
available from Dufour Editions

A Knight and His Castle

Second Edition

EWART OAKESHOTT

Superbly illustrated by the author, he
traces the design, building, and defense of
castles throughout the Middle Ages, and explores
castle armory, daily life, the training of boys
to become knights, sieges, and favorite pastimes
such as hunting and hawking.

*1996, glossary, illustrations, index, 5½ x 8½, 128 pages,
Paper ISBN 0-8023-1294-2*

TO ORDER CALL DUFOUR EDITIONS AT 1-800-869-5677

Also in the Medieval Knight series
available from Dufour Editions

A Knight and His Weapons

Second Edition

EWART OAKESHOTT

Take an engaging journey back in time, when
battles were fought with swords, lances, maces, and
an array of well-crafted devices that could be elegant
and ornate, brutal and efficient, or both. This accessi-
ble, lively, and informative book explores many
facets of the medieval world of weaponry.

1997, glossary, illustrations, index, 5½ x 8½, 128 pages,
Paper ISBN 0-8023-1299-3

TO ORDER CALL DUFOUR EDITIONS AT 1-800-869-5677

Also in the Medieval Knight series
available from Dufour Editions

A Knight in Battle

Second Edition

EWART OAKESHOTT

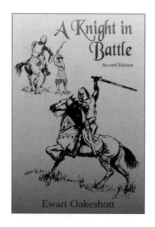

An exciting, informative look at the world
of medieval warfare. Enter an exhilarating time
of change and clashing foes in this highly readable,
authoritative exploration of a dangerous aspect
of medieval life.

*1998, glossary, illustrations, index, 5½ x 8½, 144 pages,
Paper ISBN 0-8023-1322-1*

To order call Dufour Editions at 1-800-869-5677